Columbia University

Contributions to Education

Teachers College Series

No. 790

AMS PRESS
NEW YORK

DEVELOPMENT OF THE COUNTY-UNIT SCHOOL DISTRICT IN UTAH

A Study in Adaptability

By
EDWARD ALLEN BATEMAN, Ph.D.

TEACHERS COLLEGE, COLUMBIA UNIVERSITY
CONTRIBUTIONS TO EDUCATION, NO. 790

*Published with the Approval of
Professor Paul R. Mort, Sponsor*

BUREAU OF PUBLICATIONS
TEACHERS COLLEGE, COLUMBIA UNIVERSITY
NEW YORK · 1940

Library of Congress Cataloging in Publication Data

Bateman, Edward Allen, 1895-
    Development of the county-unit school district in
Utah.

    Reprint of the 1940 ed., issued in series: Teachers
College, Columbia University. Contributions to education, no. 790.
    Originally presented as the author's thesis, Columbia.
    Bibliography: p.
    1. County school systems--Utah. I. Title. II. Se-
ries: Columbia University. Teachers College. Contributions to education, no. 790.
LB2813.B3 1972   379'.152'09752   75-176541
ISBN 0-404-55790-2

Reprinted by Special Arrangement with Teachers
College Press, New York, New York

From the edition of 1940, New York
First AMS edition published in 1972
Manufactured in the United States

AMS PRESS, INC.
NEW YORK, N. Y.   10003

ACKNOWLEDGMENTS

ALTHOUGH it would be impossible fully to acknowledge the assistance received by the author during the course of this investigation, certain sources of inspiration and assistance loom large and merit special mention. Dr. Paul R. Mort, as teacher, and as sponsor of this study, has been a source of inspiration, and a sympathetic critic during its progress. Among the members of the faculty and student body of Teachers College who have given encouragement and assistance, the author wishes especially to acknowledge the timely suggestions of Professors N. L. Engelhardt and Merle Curti of the faculty, and of Richard E. Thursfield and M. Regina Connell of the student body.

The author expresses appreciation to Charles H. Skidmore, Easton Parratt, and A. C. Matheson of the State Department of Education in Utah; to Philo T. Farnsworth, George S. Bates, A. C. Lambert, H. Parley Kilburn, and Melissa Glover for special services in the collection of data; to county clerks in sixteen Utah counties; and to numerous other residents of these counties who have given unselfishly of their time and attention in furthering the progress of this investigation.

To his wife and children who have so unselfishly cooperated in making this study possible the author wishes to express his gratitude.

E. A. B.

CONTENTS

DEVELOPMENT OF THE COUNTY-UNIT
SCHOOL DISTRICT IN UTAH

A Study in Adaptability

DEFINITIONS

THE term, *adaptation,* is used in this study with two different, though related, meanings. In the specific sense it refers to a single instance of social change, or to a new service or function not previously in use. Innovation is a synonymous term. *Adaptation,* used in the generic sense, refers to the process of adjustment of school systems to the changing social culture by the sloughing off of obsolete practices and the taking on of new services or functions to meet new needs.

Adaptability is the capacity for adaptation.

Process means a continuous social change taking place in a definite manner through the operation of forces present from the first within the situation.

County-unit school district, as used in this report, refers to an organization of the schools in which the school district is coterminous with a large part or all of a county and is the only local unit for public school administration in the territory which it serves. The terms, county-unit district, county school district, and county school district of the first class, are used synonymously in reference to the Utah situation.

CHAPTER I

BACKGROUND AND DELIMITATION OF THE PROBLEM

CONTROL OF SOCIAL CHANGE DESIRABLE

THE existence of change in all social institutions is self-evident and accepted as axiomatic by students of social problems. Changes occur in our culture through the adoption and diffusion of inventions, such invention in one part of our culture creating need for adjustment, or new invention, in other parts. In reference to this relationship Ogburn says:

Where one part of culture changes first, through some discovery or invention, and occasions changes in some part of culture dependent upon it, there frequently is a delay in the changes occasioned in the dependent part of culture. The extent of this lag will vary according to the nature of the cultural material, but may exist for a considerable number of years, during which time there may be said to be a maladjustment. It is desirable to reduce the period of maladjustment, to make the cultural adjustments as quickly as possible.[1]

The desire to minimize the evils of maladjustments in society by reducing the time elapsing between invention and diffusion of needed changes in our culture is one of the moving causes for scientific study of the processes of change in society.

NEED OF STUDY OF PROCESS OF CHANGE

Relating to desirable methods of studying these processes of change, MacIver says:

I would distinguish two broad types of causal investigation within the realm of human affairs. One we may call the historical type. Here our concern is with particular events . . . .

From the explanation of events we should distinguish the explanation of processes, of the modes of social change. In the former inquiry we are concerned with salient concrete occurrences for some reason distinguished

[1] W. F. Ogburn, *Social Change*, p. 201. New York: The Viking Press, 1928.

in the flux of change; in the latter we are concerned with the flux itself, not in its multitudinous totality, not conceived as an endless series of unique historical situations, but as a nexus of type-factors and type-situations related in a necessary or at least an understandable sequence. Because it is type-elements we are dealing with, our study belongs not to history but to social science in the strict sense. We are studying the interaction, development, reconstruction, and dissolution of social forms, procedures, and functions, or it may be the modes of adjustment of social groups to new or changing environments. To investigate these characteristic processes we must analyze individual situations, but what we are seeking to understand is why they exhibit certain characteristics or what the nexus is between them. . . . In short, what we are interested in is the nature of a social process revealed through specific situations, not these situations as concrete wholes. Otherwise we only amass information, and make the pathetic mistake of confusing it with science.[2]

According to this point of view the detailed study of specific adaptations in our culture is valuable for what it reveals as to the nature of the processes involved in social change.

STUDY OF PROCESS OF CHANGE IN EDUCATION DESIRABLE

Investigations of the processes of change in the field of education have recently been initiated by Mort and Cornell. They have found that the formulation of general principles of adaptation, the recognition of patterns of adaptability, and the identification of factors which influence adaptation depend upon the completion of a variety of specific studies in this field. Concerning this point they say:

If we are to understand adaptability, we must observe individual adaptations in all their stages. We must seek to find which factors favor and which hinder them . . . .

The precise nature of these factors, as well as a knowledge of how they are related to the adaptation process in various phases, can be discovered only by studying the life histories of many individual adaptations. This task still remains to be done.[3]

At present, several investigations in the field of adaptability in

[2] R. M. MacIver, "Causation and Social Process," Chap. XIV, pp. 140-151, in *Social Problems and Processes*, edited by Emory S. Bogardus. Chicago: University of Chicago Press, 1932.

[3] Paul R. Mort and Francis G. Cornell, *Adaptability of Public School Systems*, p. 40. New York: Teachers College, Columbia University, 1938.

education are in various stages of completion, the present study being one of these. It was undertaken for the purpose of studying the process of change operating in the adoption of a specific innovation in educational practices—to discover the pattern or patterns which the process of adaptation followed; to identify forces and factors which can be recognized as influencing this process; to identify the agencies and devices which were utilized by various forces during the process of adaptation.

REASONS FOR STUDY OF THE COUNTY-UNIT SYSTEM IN UTAH

The reasons why this specific innovation—the adoption of the county-unit district as the local unit for the administration of schools in the state of Utah—was chosen for investigation are pertinent to this report. Of primary importance is the fact that the size of local school units of administration is a significant problem in educational administration. At the present time there are approximately 127,000 local school districts in the United States, a large percentage of which have only one teacher in the district.[4] The urgent need for reorganization of the local unit for administrative purposes has been stressed by many leaders in education, of whom Cubberley could well be called representative. On this point he says:

> That the district system is wasteful of effort and funds, results in great educational waste, is unprogressive to a high degree, leads to an unwise multiplication of little schools, does not provide adequately for the needs of country and village boys and girls, and that any marked general educational progress is impossible under it, no longer admits of successful contradiction.[5]

Although several types of school administrative units have been recommended at various times by leading educators, the county-unit plan is probably the most important under consideration. One of our leading school administrators, Frank P. Graves, summarizes his analysis of the trends of school district consolidation, and the place of the county-unit plan, in the following statement:

---

[4] Walter Deffenbaugh and Timon Covert, *School Administrative Units*. United States Office of Education, Pamphlet No. 34, 1933.

[5] E. P. Cubberley, *Public Education in the United States*. Revised and Enlarged Edition, p. 72. Boston: Houghton Mifflin Co., 1934.

It can be only a matter of time before the states where the weak county-unit exists develop into the stronger organization, and before other states now upon a district or township basis, which are generally agitating the matter of a county-unit, adopt the recommendation made by Cubberley a score of years ago . . . .

[note] The history of Utah is perhaps typical of the way this will be accomplished. In 1905 a county-unit was made optional and ten years later mandatory, while errors in applying the principle have been remedied and the efficiency of the unit gradually strengthened by subsequent legislation.[6]

Additional reasons for the decision to investigate the process of adaptation involved in the adoption of the county-unit system in Utah are that the adaptation reached maturity recently enough to permit the documentary sources to be supplemented by oral testimony of persons who actively participated in the process of change and because the necessary sources for an adequate study were more readily accessible to the present investigator in Utah than in any other state having a county-unit system of schools.

PRESENT STATUS OF COUNTY-UNIT SYSTEM IN UTAH

Utah now has forty school districts and only twenty-nine counties. Each of the five first class and second class cities (7,500 population or more) is a separate school district by constitutional mandate. All other cities and villages are included in the county school districts. Four counties—Salt Lake, Utah, Sanpete, and Juab—have two school districts each, exclusive of first and second class cities. Summit County has three school districts. The creation of more than one school district in these five counties was permitted during the development of the county-unit system, either because of the large population in the counties or because of distinct differences between sections of the same county due to industrial or geographic conditions. Twenty-four counties have one school district each, coterminous with the county boundary but exclusive of any first or second class city which may be within the county limits.

The first county consolidation became effective in 1905, and in

[6] Frank P. Graves, "State and County School Administration," p. 311. Chap. X, pp. 299-326, in *Modern School Administration,* John C. Almack, Editor. Boston: Houghton Mifflin Co., 1933.

1915, after eight of the more populous counties had voluntarily consolidated, the legislature made county-unit consolidation mandatory for all counties.

SCOPE OF THIS STUDY

This investigation, therefore, is a study of the process of change involved in the adoption of the county-unit system of school districts in the state of Utah. It concerns itself with the emergence of the idea of the county unit in Utah, the development of the idea, the first adoption of the county unit, the diffusion of the adaptation, and its final maturity as a state-wide practice under mandatory law. Although the study, basically, is historical in nature, the emphasis on discovery of patterns and factors of adaptability makes it essentially a study in social change.

The investigation, then, seeks to answer the following questions:

1. What is the pattern of adaptability characteristic of the adoption of the county-unit school district in the state of Utah, as related to the invention, introduction, and diffusion of the adaptation?

2. What forces and factors appear to have influenced the adoption of the county-unit system of school districts in Utah?

3. What agencies and devices were utilized by various forces in bringing about the adaptation?

4. What are the important differences and similarities between the pattern of adaptability which operated in this adaptation and other patterns of adaptability in public school systems, as described by Cubberley, Mort, and Farnsworth?[7]

METHOD OF PROCEDURE

Statutes on education passed by the various legislative sessions of the territory and of the state of Utah, and the reports of the territorial and state superintendents of Utah, were first examined carefully for a general background of the history of the county-unit system in the state. It was found that sixteen counties in

[7] These patterns are presented in Chapter VI of this study, where the comparison is made.

Utah were eligible voluntarily to consolidate their schools on a county-unit basis at some period between 1905, when the first permissive law was passed, and 1915, when the law was made mandatory. Visits were made to each of these counties and the records of the meetings of the county commissions were examined to see what action, if any, had been taken regarding consolidation. In those counties in which some action had been taken, interviews were arranged with two or more persons in each county who had been active in the movement for or against consolidation. If any additional information was given by the persons interviewed it was checked back against written records already consulted or with additional sources which may have been suggested in the interview. Information given from memory by any person was not considered in the findings unless it agreed substantially with contemporary records or unless it was corroborated by other individuals in independent interviews and was not in conflict with reliable contemporary records. Any information depending mainly upon the memory of individuals is so indicated in the report.

SOURCES OF DATA

The principal sources of data, as indicated in the previous section, were as follows. All are listed in the Bibliography, pp. 95 to 98.

1. Published official documents of Utah—reports of the superintendents of schools of Utah territory and state; the statutes passed by the sessions of the legislatures of the territory and state of Utah; the official journals of the sessions of the legislature, the messages of the governors of the state of Utah, etc.

2. Unpublished official documents—minutes of the meetings of the county commissions; petitions presented to the county commissions; assessment rolls of the county assessors, etc.

3. Unofficial printed materials in Utah—the *Utah Educational Review*, newspaper files of various newspapers in the state, etc.

4. Interviews with individuals who participated in the process of consolidation.

5. Contemporary publications from outside the state of Utah,

such as the bulletins and reports of the United States Office of Education and contemporary periodicals.

SUMMARY

The control of change in society is desirable in order to minimize the evils of social maladjustment. To control change in society we must study the processes of change rather than isolated historical facts. Certain educators, under the leadership of Mort, have initiated studies in how adaptations take place in the field of education. Cooperating in this general field, the present investigation was made to study the process of adaptability which operated in the adoption of the county-unit system of school administration in the state of Utah. Although made primarily for the purpose of contributing to a better understanding of the general processes of adaptability in the field of education, the study may also be helpful in contributing to a better understanding of how changes occur in the specific field of school district organization.

The inquiry is limited to the process of change involved in the adoption of the county-unit system of school districts in Utah, which includes the history of the invention, the adoption, and the diffusion of the county-unit organization in that state, with special attention being given to the pattern of adaptability which the adaptation followed, the forces and factors which helped to bring it about, and the agencies and devices that were useful in the process.

Documentary sources of data for the study are supplemented by minutes of the county commissions' meetings in sixteen Utah counties and by controlled use of information received in interviews with persons who participated in the process of adaptation.

CHAPTER II

EMERGENCE AND DEVELOPMENT OF THE COUNTY-UNIT IDEA IN UTAH

DURING the year following the arrival of the Mormon colonists in Utah in 1847, the only government was that of the dominant church. After the close of the Mexican War had definitely placed the land of the Great Basin under the jurisdiction of the United States a provisional government was established and it applied to Congress for admission to the Union as the state of Deseret. Congress responded in 1850 by creating the territory of Utah.[1]

AUTHORITY TO ORGANIZE SCHOOL DISTRICTS

The early territorial legislatures organized the first settlements into counties and cities, adding additional cities or counties as the needs of expanding settlement required. The governing body of each county was the county court which, for purposes of civil government, consisted of three selectmen and the probate judge of the county, all of whom were elected at large by popular male suffrage.

Although an act was approved by the provisional legislature in 1850 creating a University of the State of Deseret, the first common school law of the territory was not approved until December 30, 1854. Certain sections of this act provided:

Sec. 2. That the county courts, in the Territory of Utah, shall at their first term hereafter, see that their respective counties are divided into suitable school districts, and shall notify the inhabitants, as soon as districts are formed, to meet within ten days, and choose three trustees . . . .

Sec. 7. Nothing in this act shall be so construed as to interfere with any of the chartered rights of any of the cities of this territory . . . .[2]

[1] Hubert Howe Bancroft, *History of Utah*, Chap. XVII, pp. 439-480. San Francisco, 1889.

[2] *Compiled Laws of Utah*, 1855, Chap. XCIV, p. 287.

8

The charters of most of the cities gave them authority to establish, support, and regulate common schools, thus making the city independent of the county in which it was located, except that the authority did not extend to consolidating school districts. By an amendment to the law in 1866, this power was delegated by the legislature to the county courts only.

The county courts are hereby empowered to change the boundaries of school districts, or consolidate two or more into one, if the public good require . . . .[3]

This authority of the county court to create, alter, or consolidate school districts was continued throughout the history of Utah as a territory, but after Utah became a state in 1896, it was given, unchanged, to the county commission which replaced the county court as the chief governing body of the county.

In addition to using the county as an agency in the creation of school districts, it appears to have been the intention of the early territorial government of Utah to use the county as the unit of supervision. The revised school law of 1866[4] provided for the election by popular vote of a county superintendent of schools, who was to have important powers of supervision over trustees, teachers, and distribution of school funds, but the failure to give this officer any real authority over the appointment of teachers or the raising of school funds prevented him from becoming the coordinating school officer of the county. The fact soon became evident that no central county agency had authority effectively to coordinate the essential functions of the local school districts.

INCREASE IN NUMBER OF LOCAL SCHOOL DISTRICTS

Meanwhile these local districts rapidly increased in number. The provision in the law that the county court may create new school districts whenever petitioned by parents of twenty or more children who were living two or more miles from an existing school seems to have been interpreted as a mandatory provision. Reports of territorial superintendents of common schools show that there were 186 districts in 1867, 224 districts in 1874, 318

---

[3] *Compiled Laws of Utah,* 1866, Chap. CLXII, p. 219.
[4] *Ibid.,* Chap. CLXII.

districts in 1883, and 334 districts in 1890. These increases took place despite the consolidations which were being made in the cities during this period, as is explained in a later section of this chapter.

Throughout this period of multiplication of school districts, authority remained with the chief governing body of the county to reduce, rather than to increase, the number of local administrative school units if it had thought it desirable so to do.

EXPRESSION OF NEED OF LARGER SCHOOL DISTRICTS

Practically from the beginning of settlement in Utah, leaders in government and education recognized that the common school system was in need of improvement. In his message to the legislature, dated December 11, 1854, Governor Young said:

As a territory we have peace, and extensive ability exists with the people, to establish and sustain good common schools in every ward and district, not only three, or six months in a year, as appears at present most common; but ten or eleven wherein every child, no matter how poor, may find admittance. Schools for teachers, mathematical schools, and schools wherein the higher branches are taught, should also be kept in successful operation, in all the principal towns.[5]

Such a system, however, was not established. By 1867 the schools of the territory were kept open, on an average, less than six months in the year. Tuition fees ranged from three to six dollars per quarter for pupils in the common English branches.[6] Not only were the schools open for only part of the year but many of the children of the territory did not attend school. As late as 1875, the reports of the territorial superintendent show that only 54 per cent of the children of the territory were enrolled in school and the average daily attendance was equal to approximately 40 per cent of the children of school age.[7] Since the tuition fees were supplemented only by a small county and local tax, the source of support was local in character and the length of the

[5] *Journal of the Legislative Assembly of the Territory of Utah*, 1854-55. Great Salt Lake City, 1855.
[6] *Annual Report of the Territorial Superintendent of Common Schools*, 1867, p. 3.
[7] *Biennial Report of the Territorial Superintendent of Common Schools*, 1874 and 1875, p. 4.

school year was dependent upon the amount of local taxable wealth and the willingness of the localities to tax themselves.

SUGGESTED REASONS FOR NEED OF LARGER DISTRICTS

Suggestions for a better system of schools early began to appear, of which the following two are important:

It is respectfully submitted whether the territorial tax should not be increased one fourth of one per cent, and that this amount be appropriated for the use of the common schools, also that it be enacted that the tax collected by the counties from railroads, and the licenses by cities from banks, inure to the school fund. And it is further submitted whether the school fund is not the more proper to receive all fines, forfeitures, and escheats.[8]

In 1875 Superintendent Riggs made this recommendation:

The cities, towns, villages, and settlements of our Territory are well adapted for the establishment of the system of graded schools. Places that now have two, three, four, or five small school houses, and as many mixed schools in which but little comparatively can be accomplished, should have but one large commodious public school house in a central location, and containing a sufficient number of rooms that all the children of the places could be admitted into the grade for which they are qualified. I, therefore, earnestly recommend the adoption of this system throughout the territory, wherever consistent with the school population, not only as a matter of accommodation to all the children, but also as a matter of economy. By the adoption of this system, our entire school-population could be instructed in the graded schools at but little more expense than we now have to educate forty-five per cent.[9]

Two fundamental needs affected by the size of school districts are expressed in the foregoing statements: (1) the need for a larger unit of taxation than the local district, and (2) the need for more children in each school than were contained in a one-teacher district, in order to permit gradation of pupils for purposes of instruction.

The suggestion for a source of income from territorial and county-wide areas arose from Superintendent Campbell's desire to provide free schools. He realized that many of the local school

---

[8] *Biennial Report of the Territorial Superintendent of Common Schools*, 1871, p. 1.
[9] Biennial School Report, 1875, *op. cit.*, p. 6.

districts could not provide free schools for a desirable length of term each year if they must depend upon local sources of revenue. The legislature of 1874 carried out the suggestion for a territorial tax by providing for a fund of $15,000 each year for distribution to the school districts on a per capita basis, which was increased to $20,000 per year in 1876. In 1878 this was changed to the proceeds from a three mill tax, considerably increasing the amount. Campbell's suggestion to levy a county tax on railroads and banks, the proceeds of which should be distributed on a per capita basis to the children of the whole county, resulted in 1876 in the passage of such a law, as applied to the railroads, but the tax was declared unconstitutional by the supreme court of the territory.

The need for larger school districts in order to permit the gradation of schools was urged, not only by Superintendent Riggs, but by other educators also. In 1879 John R. Park, president of the University of Deseret, and L. F. Moench, county superintendent of district schools of Weber County, visited schools in the northern counties of the territory and reported to the territorial superintendent that,

The grading of schools is a subject of which we took particular note and urged on almost every occasion in speaking before the people.[10]

CONSOLIDATION OF SCHOOL DISTRICTS IN CITIES

The first consolidations of school districts for the purpose of securing better schools took place in the cities. When charters were first granted to cities by the legislature, school districts were already in existence in those cities, usually one school district for each church congregation, or "ward," in the city.[11] When the city governments were organized they allowed the districts to remain as they were, probably because the definite power to consolidate districts was not given to the cities.

The first mention in the reports of the superintendent of common schools for the territory, of the desirability of consolidating

[10] Biennial Report of the Territorial Superintendent of District Schools, 1878 and 1879, p. 9.
[11] Minutes of Cache County Court, December 6, 1864.

the city school districts, is contained in Superintendent Campbell's report of 1871:

It is maintained by some of our educators that the trustees in cities should be relieved by educational boards, whose secretary should be city superintendent.[12]

This was followed by a more definite recommendation in the reports of 1873 and of 1875. In 1878 Governor Emery made a definite recommendation to the legislature that the school districts in the cities should be combined.[13]

Logan was the first city to consolidate its districts, when, in 1872, it combined five school districts under one board of education. County court records of the counties show that Provo did likewise in 1875; St. George in 1877; Fillmore and Ogden in 1878; and Beaver in 1881. In two of these instances the county court records give the reasons for the consolidations. Under date of December 2, 1878, the Millard County Court minutes contain the following statement:

Petitions were received from the school districts of Fillmore, viz., 1st District, 30 signers; 2nd District with 44 signers; 3rd District with 29 signers; 4th District with 22 signers, asking that the four districts of this city be consolidated for the purpose of facilitating the establishing of a graded school system. The petition was granted and the four districts of Fillmore were declared one.[14]

The reasons given in the Ogden consolidation are somewhat different, stressing the practical difficulties of maintaining separate school districts in a growing city.

Your committee to whom was referred the several petitions of D. H. Peery and 57 others, Barnard White and 26 others, and Robt. McQuarrie and 50 others asking the court to consolidate the First, Second, and Third School Districts of Weber County, respectfully beg leave to report that after due consideration of the subject matter of said petitions, it appears to your committee that by granting the prayer of the petitioners a more equal and just apportionment of taxes would be secured to the entire city of Ogden, while the cost of collecting would be materially lessened, as one Board of Trustees and one assessor and collector could then be

[12] Biennial School Report, 1871, *op. cit.*, p. 3.
[13] *Journal of the Twenty-Third Session of the Legislative Assembly of the Territory of Utah*, 1878, p. 33.
[14] Minutes of Millard County Court, 1878.

uniform throughout the city, while heretofore it has varied in the several districts so much that while one district was obliged to assess three per cent, another could accomplish as much with a tax of one per cent, or even less, and it frequently happens that taxpayers reside in one district while their property is mainly situated in another, thus compelling them to send their children out of the district in which they reside, in order to realize the benefits of the taxes which they pay. For the foregoing and other reasons which your committee do not deem it necessary to enumerate we recommend that the prayer of the petitioners be granted.[15]

Ogden, January 15th, 1878   L. J. Herrick ⎫
                                   R. Ballantyne ⎭ Committee

By 1882 no city in the territory of Utah had more than one school district within its boundaries except Salt Lake City, which did not consolidate its twenty separate school districts until required to do so by the passage of the revised free school law of 1890. In the meantime, through the reports of the territorial superintendent and visits to local districts by him and his representatives, the advantages gained by the cities as a result of district consolidations were presented to the people in other sections of the state.[16]

That these attempts on the part of educators to secure graded schools were successful in so far as the larger communities of the state are concerned is shown by a comparison of the number of school districts in each community[17] with the population figures of those communities for the year 1900.[18] Of the thirty-seven incorporated cities, towns, and villages listed in the census data for that year, as having a population of 1,000 or more, only one had more than one school district within its boundaries. Examination of the available reports of the county superintendents and of the state superintendents of schools from 1870 to 1900 shows that central schools had been erected in practically all of these larger villages and cities which had a school population of approximately 300 or more.

[15] Minutes of Weber County Court, January 15, 1878.

[16] *Biennial Report of Territorial Superintendent of Common Schools*, 1881, 1883, and 1887.

[17] *Third Report of the Superintendent of Public Instruction of the State of Utah*, 1900, pp. 368-78.

[18] *Twelfth Census of the United States*, 1900, Vol. I, p. 477.

Although these central schools were of adequate size to provide fairly efficient instruction, the school districts in all cities except four—Salt Lake City, Ogden, Provo, and Logan—were dependent upon a small area for local tax-income; they were organized and conducted under the local district trustee system; and practically none of them were large enough to maintain high schools.

Of the 380 local school districts in the state in 1900, 180, or 47 per cent, had less than 100 children of school age in the district, while 271 districts, or 71 per cent, had a school population of less than 200 children.

It is evident from these data that the consolidation of districts in the larger towns had not removed the need for a larger unit of administration for the rural schools in Utah.

EMERGENCE OF THE COUNTY-UNIT IDEA

The first known recommendation that county units for local school administration should be created in Utah is that found in the biennial school report for the period ending June 30, 1881. Superintendent L. John Nuttall had requested John R. Park, president of the University of Deseret, and M. H. Hardy, superintendent of schools in Utah County, to visit schools in the northern part of the territory. In their report of these visits the following statements appear:

We found a disposition in some places to divide up the school districts for insufficient cause; nothing can be more detrimental than this, to any scheme of gradation, to effective supervision or, in fact, to organization. . . .

Consolidation gives better schoolhouses, better qualified teachers, more and better furniture and apparatus, better gradation, and much less expense. We hope that our efforts had some effect in arresting this tendency to multiply small and weak districts.[19]

District organization would naturally lead to county organization, and this as naturally grow into an efficient state organization where there is no permanent provision to support it. We are convinced that a plan making each county a district, with a board of five or six trustees, would give us a much more effective school system; such a plan has many arguments in its favor and is worthy the consideration of our legislature.

[19] *Biennial Report of the Territorial Superintendent of District Schools*, 1881, p. 36.

It could be adopted as an amendment to our present school law, without producing any abrupt or violent changes.[20]

It should be noted that Park and Hardy made these visits together and that the report does not indicate which one first suggested the county-unit plan. Evidence is not available to the present investigator as to which man really made the suggestion, but developments show that it was Park who subsequently championed the idea vigorously and placed it before the people of the territory.

The next known public mention of the county-unit plan was in 1888 when James H. Moyle introduced a bill into the house of representatives of the territory, which provided for the consolidation and organization of all school districts in the territory, except in cities of more than 5,000 population, into county school districts. Local newspaper comment establishes the fact that the school organization provided by the bill was that known to be advocated by John R. Park.[21]

The county board of education proposed by this measure was to consist of five members, two of whom were to be appointed annually by the county court and three of whom were to be elected from the county at large, in the same manner as the selectmen. One of the three elected members was to be known as the county superintendent of district schools and to be so elected. The board was to consider, determine, and execute all matters pertaining to the interests of public school education in each county school district. Among other powers, it was to have authority to establish one or more intermediate and high schools at advantageous points in the county.

The measure was vigorously attacked by the leading newspaper of Salt Lake City. The charges were that the measure was carelessly prepared; that legislative powers were given to the county board of education; that the right was given to each county to establish free schools by a majority vote of the electors, rather than by the property owners; and that the board had unlimited power to establish high schools which were to be located in certain

[20] Biennial School Report, 1881, *op. cit.*, p. 28.
[21] *Deseret Evening News,* January 30 to February 2, 1888.

school districts, but which were to be paid for with taxes from all school districts.[22] Although the newspaper declared it was not opposed to the general purposes of the bill it is significant that the measure was not reported from the committee and that no other bill on education considered at that session contained the county-unit provision. After the failure of this proposed law to receive serious consideration by the legislature, no other educational measure providing for the county-unit plan appears to have come before the legislature until 1905.

PROPOSED CHANGES IN COUNTY-UNIT PLAN

Two interesting variations of the county-unit idea were contained in the territorial school reports of 1891 and 1895. Superintendent Boreman suggested that the plan be made optional for each county upon popular vote.

It is deemed by some that the school law would be greatly improved by the creation of county school boards, with the county superintendents as chairmen of such boards, and that such county boards should assume the powers and discharge the duties now developing upon district school boards and school trustees. If the law-making power should deem it wise to change the school law in this regard, it would probably be well to leave the adoption or rejection of the change to a vote of the people of each county, such vote to be taken upon the order of the county court whenever a proper petition is presented therefor. Some counties may be ready for such change and others may not.[23]

In the 1895 biennial report, Superintendent Lewis made a recommendation to the legislature for a different type of consolidation.

One more suggestion, and I ask that you consider it seriously. It is the proposition to do away entirely with our present district organization and establish in place thereof the township organization.

For data, I refer you to a most thorough and careful collection of facts and arguments, collected and prepared by State Superintendent Poland of New Jersey, and which is on file in the office of the State Superintendent of Utah.[24]

[22] *Ibid.*

[23] *Biennial Report of the Commissioner of Schools for Utah Territory,* 1890 and 1891, p. 9.

[24] *Biennial Report of the Commissioner of Schools for Utah Territory,* 1894 and 1895, p. 14.

Since Utah did not have a system of township government this recommendation is difficult to understand except as it may be partially explained by the following extract from a letter of Superintendent Lewis to Superintendent Poland of New Jersey:

> . . . I have advocated the doctrine of uniting all the county districts into one, to be under the supervision of a county board of education. This would enable the board to establish a system of graded schools with a central or high school for the county . . . . I am mindful of the fact that the population of our most populous counties will demand several high schools to the county, and consequently a more perfect system of grading. Therefore, I am persuaded that the township is large enough to obtain all the privileges desired and with the least cost for the product . . . .[25]

Lewis seems to have been recommending a plan of creating several districts in each of the more populous counties, corresponding to the number of high schools needed in the county. It appears that this variation of the county-unit idea previously suggested by Park and Boreman was due to the influence of the New Jersey report. It will be noted in Chapter III that this was the plan Superintendent Ashton of Salt Lake County had in mind when he made his recommendation, in 1904, to consolidate that county into eight school districts.

PARK'S REPORT OF 1896

In the meantime, Congress had authorized the admission of Utah into the Union as a state and John R. Park had been elected as the first superintendent of public instruction of the state of Utah, to take office in January of 1896.

A year after assuming office Park issued his first report as state superintendent of schools, in which he went into a detailed explanation of a proposed county-unit system and its advantages. He listed some advantages of the township plan as tried in several eastern states, and referred to a collection of opinions and arguments advanced for the township system published in the report of the New York department of public instruction for 1889. He then stated:

[25] *Annual Report of the Board of Education and of the Superintendent of Public Instruction of New Jersey*, 1894, Appendix, p. xix.

I urge at this time that the adoption of this plan be seriously considered for our schools, to be known to us as the county or county district plan, as the county is the lowest available civil unit for us.[26]

Park quoted arguments of Superintendent Van Cott of Salt Lake County and of Superintendent Wootton of Wasatch County in favor of establishing county school districts. He also referred to the experience of the large school districts in the first and second class cities of the state in securing efficient systems of graded schools since 1890, when the city school laws had been revised and city school superintendents had been appointed in each city. He summarized the arguments for the proposed plan by listing twenty-four reasons why it would be preferable to the district system, and then concluded as follows:

It has been suggested that the same system if necessary could be carried out on a voluntary plan, that is "Let those counties wishing to organize their schools this way, agree among themselves to do so." Experience has proven that no system however meritorious or well adapted to the circumstances to which it is applied, can be made to operate successfully if dependent at every step in its execution on the precarious judgment or whim of the populace. It must have, to insure success, a law that will not only clearly define its plan and mode of execution, but enforce compliance therewith.[27]

The plan of organization for the county school district recommended in this report was different in several essential respects from the plan suggested in the Moyle bill introduced into the legislature of 1888. One difference was that the 1888 plan provided for a local district trustee who should take the census each year and perform certain custodial services in the care of the local school property. The 1896 plan would eliminate all local district organization. A second difference was that the 1896 plan would have the superintendent and clerk appointed by and responsible to the board of education. The earlier plan provided for the superintendent of schools to be elected by the people and to be chairman of the board. It is highly probable that these differences appeared in Park's later plan because of the experience

[26] *First Report of the State Superintendent of Public Instruction of the State of Utah,* 1896, p. 18.
[27] *Ibid.,* p. 26.

of the first and second class cities of Utah with the type of organization he now recommended. Park cites the experience of these cities to argue that a similar organization would bring equally desirable results in the counties outside of the cities.

GROWTH OF COUNTY-UNIT IDEA

Following the circulation of the 1896 report, county superintendents began to suggest in their biennial reports to the state superintendent that the county-unit plan should be adopted. Four county reports recommended the plan in 1898, two recommended it in 1900, ten advocated the plan in 1902, and twelve urged the adoption of the county unit in their reports of 1904.[28] Between 1896 and 1904 inclusive, the superintendents of nineteen different counties made this recommendation to the state office, urging that either a mandatory or a permissive law be passed by the legislature.

Although Governor Heber M. Wells in his messages to the legislatures of 1902 and 1903 recommended the creation of county-unit school districts, no action appears to have been taken by these legislatures to carry out the recommendations.

Meanwhile, in his report for the biennial period ending June 30, 1898, Park urged that if a mandatory law could not be passed, a permissive law should be enacted.

If the law be not changed so as to consolidate all the districts in each county, there should be a definite provision making it optional with the people in each county to so unite if they choose. This would probably effect, gradually, the much needed reform that we have so far been unable to effect all at once.[29]

It is evident from this statement, in view of his previous stand in favor of a state-wide mandatory law, that Park was losing faith in the possibility of getting such a sweeping reform by one act of the legislature and was willing to take the slower way of gradual change that would be possible under an optional law.

However, Park refused to compromise on the idea of having

---

[28] See Biennial State School Reports for the years 1898, 1900, 1902, and 1904.
[29] *Second Report of the Superintendent of Public Instruction of the State of Utah,* 1898, p. 46.

only one school board for each county and giving it complete control of the schools. On this point he says:

> While many are opposed to making the counties units of organization and administration, as well as of supervision in school matters, they at the same time favor making the county, and even the State, the smallest unit of taxation: That is, they desire to retain local power without local responsibility . . . . Whatever system we adopt, power and responsibility must not be separated. To separate them would be to violate the fundamental principle of public economy, and to bring upon our schools the numerous ills of incompetency and corruption engendered by a vicious system.[30]

Park died in 1900 and his successor in office recommended an optional consolidation law in the state school report for that year. Although Park had definitely established the idea of the county unit for Utah schools he did not live to see the plan actually in operation. The extent to which he had supported the idea and its apparent failure at the time of his death are shown in the following passage from a short biography of Dr. Park, written by William G. Roylance:

> His efforts while superintendent were directed chiefly towards the reforming of school administration. In his attempts to secure a uniform system of administration and supervision throughout the state, by the consolidation of districts under county boards, he failed; but many who at first strenuously opposed the plan now see the wisdom of it, and though local sentiment is perhaps too strong to ever admit this reform, those who knew Dr. Park, and heard him explain it, know out of what high aims and unselfish devotion to the cause of education it was conceived.[31]

WAS COUNTY-UNIT IDEA INDIGENOUS?

The inquiry as to where Park and Hardy got the idea of a county-unit organization which they recommended in 1881 may never be satisfactorily answered. Later developments have usually caused Park's name to be associated with the emergence of the idea, but whether it grew naturally out of the existing organization of the county as a unit for supervisory purposes and the need

---

[30] *Ibid.*, p. 26.
[31] *Third Report of the Superintendent of Public Instruction of the State of Utah,* 1900, p. 44.

for larger units of organization and administration, or whether it had been suggested to Park from outside sources, is not clear. Park had received a Bachelor's degree from the Ohio Wesleyan University in 1853, and a degree of Doctor of Medicine from the University of the City of New York in 1857. He was an instructor at Ohio Wesleyan University until 1860 and left for the West in 1861.[32] He became president of the University of Deseret in Salt Lake City in 1869, and in 1871 went to Europe for a year, during which time he visited schools and studied methods of instruction.[33] His experience, therefore, was broad and his opportunities to become acquainted with different types of educational organization were many. Moreover, one state, Maryland, had adopted the county-unit organization in 1865 and Park probably had opportunity to become acquainted with this fact through the reports of the United States Commissioner of Education.

On the other hand, if Park had known that the county-unit plan was in operation in any state in 1881, it is difficult to understand why he did not refer to that fact as additional evidence for its adoption. Even in 1896, when he made his principal argument for the county unit, in his search for reasons why the plan should be successful in Utah he turned to the experience of the north Atlantic states with the township plan[34] and seemed to be ignorant of the existence of the county-unit plan in the southern states of Maryland, Louisiana, North Carolina, Georgia, and Florida.[35]

Although his experience outside of Utah had been fairly extensive, absence of any reference to the county-unit organization in other states, either in the 1881 report or in that of 1896, makes it probable that the idea was indigenous, especially since so many of the essential elements of the county-unit plan were present in the Utah school situation as it existed in 1881.

Another factor to be considered is the fact that Park made visits to the counties of northern Utah at two different times, once

[32] Levi Edgar Young, *Dr. John Rocky Park*, Salt Lake City, 1919.

[33] Biennial School Report, 1875, *op. cit.*, pp. 45-46.

[34] First State School Report, 1896, *op. cit.*, p. 18.

[35] Cubberley, E. P., *State School Administration*, Chap. X. Boston: Houghton Mifflin Co., 1927.

in 1879 and once in 1881, with a different companion on each trip.[36] Since mention of the county-unit idea was not made until the report of 1881, it may give credibility to the argument that his companion of that year, M. H. Hardy, was responsible for the idea. A biography of Hardy does not seem to exist so that data are lacking on which to base judgment. However, in the absence of good evidence to the contrary, if the county-unit idea emerged from the local situation, it is probably fair to assume that it originated with the man who fought for it from that day to the end of his life, John R. Park.

THE HIGH SCHOOL PROBLEM

It is probable that one of the major factors which eventually brought about the adoption of the county-unit system in Utah was the growing need for high schools in the rural areas. In 1884 the school law was amended to permit any school district which had a population of more than 1,200, when authorized by a majority vote of the property taxpayers resident in the district, to maintain a graded school or department in which pupils might be instructed in higher branches of education than those usually taught in the common schools, and permit children more than eighteen years of age to attend such a school. The population limit of 1,200 for authority to establish a high school was raised to 1,500 in 1892, at which time authority also was given for school trustees of two or more contiguous districts to form a union district for the purpose of establishing a high school. In 1897 the law was amended to require a majority vote of the electors before such a high school district could be created. In 1901 the law was again amended to permit any district with a population of 1,000 or more to establish a high school subject to approval by a vote of the electors in the district.

These laws did not prove effective in securing the establishing of high schools where they were needed. By 1904 there were only eleven counties, exclusive of the cities, that offered public high school work of any kind and the high schools in these counties were maintained by small towns that could not afford to support

[36] Biennial School Report, 1879, *op. cit.*, p. 9.

a creditable high school program. Only three counties offered work in the eleventh grade, in which there was a combined enrollment of twenty-two students, and a twelfth grade was conducted in only one county, with an enrollment of six pupils. In 1904 the thirty-six rural school districts of Salt Lake County had a school enrollment of 6,954 children, 330 of whom were registered in the eighth grade. The high school enrollment, however, was only twenty-two, eighteen in the ninth grade and four in the tenth grade.[37] Most graduates of the eighth grade could not attend high school unless they paid tuition and living expenses to attend school in a city.

School leaders repeatedly suggested to state officials and to the state legislature that the situation was deplorable but that little improvement could be expected under the existing school organization and school law. Oscar Van Cott, superintendent of schools of Salt Lake County, commented in his report of 1900:

The establishment of county high schools is impossible under the present law and district system.[38]

Two years later, B. W. Ashton, who was Van Cott's successor, commented as follows:

The formation of one county board would be the greatest step in advance our school could take. It would settle the matter of gradation of the high school and give a dignity and tone to the schools that would place them on an entirely new and higher plane.[39]

State Superintendent A. C. Nelson called the attention of the legislature to the backward condition of the high schools in his report of 1902:

At the beginning of the last biennial period, there were but five public high schools in the State, including those in the cities of the first and of the second class. Careful investigation showed that scarcely another State of the Union was so deficient in this part of its school system. County superintendents, as well as many of the people at large, felt that the time had come to strengthen the link between the common schools and the college, and to furnish an opportunity to the boys and

---

[37] *Fifth Report of the Superintendent of Public Instruction of the State of Utah,* 1904, Statistical Section.
[38] Biennial State School Report, 1900, *op. cit.,* p. 274.
[39] Biennial State School Report, 1902, *op. cit.,* p. 230.

the girls who cannot well go off to college, to receive some higher instruction at home, so when suggestions went out for action in this matter, the superintendents worked with commendable zeal for the establishment of high schools in their counties. In Salt Lake and in other counties meetings were held at which the superintendents, professors of the State University, and other leading educators set forth the desirability and feasibility of creating and maintaining schools for higher instruction. As a result of these efforts, there are today nineteen public high schools in Utah . . . .

There are conditions militating against the public rural high school which might easily be remedied . . . . The children of poor districts are entitled to the advantages of higher learning as well as those in districts with wealth at their command. But of this privilege they are and will be denied unless some additional means of financial assistance is given the district. If a county were but one school district, governed by a thoroughly competent board of education, the board might say: We will establish a high school here, or we will have a high school there and it would be done. But if the consolidation of districts is not effected, then I am of the opinion that the State will have to lend support to the rural high school before it becomes a strong and permanent force in our commonwealth.[40]

Stimulated by the campaign for establishing of high schools, which had been conducted in Salt Lake County under the leadership of State Superintendent A. C. Nelson, the school leaders of Salt Lake County arranged during the year 1903 for the people to vote on the creation of a county high school district. Under the law, every district within the contiguous territory to be included in the high school district must vote favorably or it could not be included. The failure to secure favorable vote in strategically located districts is commented upon by Superintendent Ashton in his 1904 report as follows:

As the high school [law] now stands it is practically a dead letter. One indisposed district can hold back high school facilities from the most ambitious of surrounding districts, as was recently demonstrated in Salt Lake County when the people voted on the high school question. Although the great majority of the districts voted in favor of a county high school the districts were not all in favor of the measure and the proposition failed to carry.

The great needs of our county, in fact, of the entire state, are proper high school facilities. Many pupils who graduate from the public schools

[40] Biennial State School Report, 1902, *op. cit.*, p. 22.

are not financially able to pursue their studies further, and are therefore deprived of the needed instruction to fit them for life. Besides, many
pupils who go to schools in large cities are weaned from their country
homes, and culture and refinement are gradually drawn from the
country schools into such cities . . . .[41]

At the opening of the year 1904, therefore, the people of rural
Salt Lake County were practically without public high schools.
They had recently failed to carry an election for the creation of
a county high school district according to the requirements of
the existing law, and practically none of the local school districts
had adequate population and resources to maintain a high school
alone. In respect to these handicaps of organization and wealth,
many other counties were in no more favorable position to establish high schools than was the county of Salt Lake.

SUMMARY

When the civil government of Utah territory was established,
the county was made the unit for local administration. To the
chief governing body of the county was given the power to create,
alter, or consolidate school districts within the county. By 1905
this authority, in its essential features, remained with the county
commissioners of each county in the state.

The many small local school districts proved burdensome in
the cities because of practical difficulties encountered by the
existence of many separate taxing units within a densely populated area. Beginning with Logan in 1872, in all of the larger
cities, except in Salt Lake City, the school trustees and citizens
petitioned the county courts to consolidate the districts within
each city. These consolidations were made. In 1890 Salt Lake
City was forced to follow the example of the other cities by mandatory state law.

The success of the centralized school system in the cities caused
educational leaders to seek ways to secure similar benefits for
rural schools. Although they were successful in securing a uniform
territorial tax, it failed materially to correct weaknesses due to
faulty organization.

[41] Biennial State School Report, 1904, *op. cit.*, p. 135.

The first mention of a plan to remedy the inherent weakness of the local district system was made in 1881, probably by John R. Park, when he advocated the consolidation of all the local districts within a county into one school district to be governed by one county board of education.

An attempt was made in 1888 to secure the adoption of this county-unit system for the entire territory by mandatory law, but the effort failed. Two variations of the county-unit organization were soon suggested. One suggestion was that legal permission be granted to counties to adopt voluntarily the county-unit idea, and the other provided for the creation of several districts within each county.

In 1896 John R. Park, upon his election to the position of State Superintendent of Public Instruction, began a vigorous agitation for the adoption of the county-unit school system. County school superintendents began to support him in his request for the passage of mandatory or permissive legislation for establishing the proposed county district, but at the time of Park's death in 1900 the enactment of the desired legislation appeared to be no more probable than it had been in 1888. However, during the next four years there was a rapid increase in the number of county superintendents who recommended changes in district organization.

The increased interest in consolidation at this time was probably due to the need for high school facilities in the rural districts of the state and to the financial inability of small school districts to support an adequate high school program. The state law permitted contiguous districts to unite for the purpose of maintaining a high school, provided the plan was approved by a majority vote of electors in each district. Attempts to form union high schools under this law had proved unsuccessful.

ANALYTICAL SUMMARY STATEMENTS

In appraising the process of the invention and development of the county-unit plan, as related to its status in 1904, the following statements appear to be justified:

1. The formation of independent school districts in each of the

first and second class cities had, to a great extent, lessened the immediate interest of the city populations in the solution of the county school problems.

2. The consolidation of the school districts within each of the smaller cities and larger towns of the counties had the effect of temporarily decreasing their immediate interest in the formation of a county-unit school district. This probably is a reason why the plan did not receive widespread support prior to 1900.

3. The county-unit plan was first suggested in 1881 by an agent of the territorial school office. Until 1896 efforts for the development of the plan appear to have been made principally by officials of the territorial school office or of the University of Deseret.

4. From the emergence of the county-unit idea in 1881 until 1904, all supporters of the plan had assumed that the first step necessary for its adoption was the enactment of a mandatory or a permissive law by the legislature.

5. The need for establishing a system of rural high schools in Utah appeared by 1904 to demand some modification of the district school organization.

6. Although twenty-three years after the emergence of the county-unit idea its adoption did not appear to be probable, the fact that it was being widely advocated by educational leaders during the period from 1900 to 1904 would tend to place it in a position of first consideration in the adoption of any plan for consolidation of school districts which might be attempted in order to solve the high school problem.

CHAPTER III

THE FIRST ADOPTION AND THE COUNTY
DISTRICT LAW

THE populated area of Salt Lake County consists of a valley approximately twenty miles long and ten miles wide at the south end, widening gradually to the north until it becomes about twenty miles wide. It is entirely surrounded by mountains except in the northwest where it opens out upon the barren shores of Great Salt Lake. Salt Lake City is at the northeastern edge of the valley, part of it being located on the foothills of the mountains to the north and east. The populated section of the county lies within a fan-shaped area of twenty-five miles radius from the center of Salt Lake City. In 1904 the Salt Lake City school district was independent of the county school system and was organized under laws that applied to school districts in cities of the first and second class.

DEFECTS OF SALT LAKE COUNTY SCHOOL ORGANIZATION

For some time prior to 1904 certain factors had been contributing to an increase in maladjustment between the school districts of rural Salt Lake County and the communities which they served. Three of these factors were: (1) the rapid increase in the population of the rural sections of the county; (2) the lack of adjustment in school district boundaries or organization; and (3) the need for more adequate high school facilities.

Between 1890 and 1900 the population of Salt Lake County, outside of Salt Lake City, increased from 13,614 to 24,194, a gain of 79 per cent. During the same period the increase of population in Salt Lake City was 19 per cent and the increase of population for the state was 33 per cent.[1] From 1892 to 1904, dates for which comparable figures are available, the school population in rural

[1] *Twelfth Census of the United States,* 1900, Vol. 1, p. 393.

Salt Lake County, for children six to eighteen years of age, increased from 5,249 to 8,739, or 66 per cent.[2] An examination of the census reports on population increases for minor civil subdivisions of the county shows that the increase in population took place in a fairly uniform way throughout the county.

During this period of increase in population of the rural sections of the county, practically no change was made in school district boundaries. In 1891 there were thirty-six school districts in Salt Lake County, outside of Salt Lake City, and the report of 1904 shows the same number of districts. An examination of reports which give the names of districts shows that very little change was made in district organization between 1883 and 1896, except to create four new districts in remote sections of the county or to change the names of several districts, and that practically no change was made between 1896 and 1904. This situation would indicate that as the population and wealth of the county had grown no adjustments of school district boundaries had been made to secure more equitable distribution of taxable wealth or to make school services more accessible and convenient for the children.

As explained in Chapter II, the public high school facilities in rural Salt Lake County in 1904 were limited to some ninth and tenth grade subjects taught by interested teachers in two local districts.[3] In general, a high school education was available only to those children whose parents were financially able and willing to send them to private or public high schools in Salt Lake City. One reason for this lack of high school facilities may have been the absence in rural Salt Lake County of school districts of sufficient size to support a high school. In 1900 only one rural Salt Lake County community was included in the list of incorporated villages, towns, and cities of the state.[4] This was Sandy, with a population of only 1,030. In 1904 the town of Murray, which was incorporated a year later as a second class city with a population of 5,000, was divided into three separate school

2 Biennial State School Report, 1893 and 1904, *op. cit.*
3 *Deseret Evening News*, August 6, 1904.
4 *Twelfth Census of the United States*, 1900, Vol. I, p. 393.

districts. Bingham, the largest community next to Murray, was divided into two school districts. Under these conditions the establishing of public high schools in Salt Lake County did not appear to be possible until some form of consolidation of existing school districts had been effected.

EARLY EFFORTS TO REMEDY DEFECTS

The first superintendent of schools in Salt Lake County to recognize the weaknesses of the rural school organization, and to recommend a plan for improvement, was Oscar Van Cott, who made the following recommendation in his report of 1896:

Not all children enjoy the same advantages, not all schools run for the same length of time, not all taxpayers pay the same rate—all these would find remedy in a consolidation of districts, controlled by a board of education.

District boundary lines prevent children, in many instances, from attending the school nearest them and they are compelled to walk a mile or two to their own school.

High schools are needed. No single district could maintain one, and local interests prevent the union of two or more districts in the establishing and supporting of such institutions . . . .

I recommend, therefore, a school bill providing for the consolidation of all districts in counties like Salt Lake County into a single district, whose schools are to be maintained and controlled by a board of education.[5]

In 1900 B. W. Ashton succeeded Van Cott as county superintendent of schools and continued to advocate consolidation and to stress the need for high schools. As pointed out in Chapter II, there was a rapid increase, after 1900, in sentiment for establishing county school districts. The governor recommended to the legislature in 1901 and in 1903 that a county school district law should be enacted, but the legislature did not take action. Apparently despairing of securing the establishment of high schools by organization of county school districts, State Superintendent A. C. Nelson in 1902 and 1903 organized a state-wide campaign for the establishing of high schools in the larger towns. In rural Salt Lake County, however, there were no large school districts,

---

[5] Biennial State School Report, 1896, *op. cit.*, p. 94.

so Superintendent Ashton attempted to organize a county high school district by popular vote, as required by law. The attempt was unsuccessful.

ASHTON'S RECOMMENDATION TO COUNTY COMMISSION

Ashton[6] now turned to the authority to consolidate local school districts which the law gave to the county and which had recently been reaffirmed in an opinion of the attorney general.[7] He devised a plan for consolidating the thirty-six school districts of the county into eight school districts with the intent that each of these districts should establish a high school.[8] Under date of January 12, 1904, he submitted his plan to the county commission, which considered the recommendation at a meeting on January 18, took it under advisement, and immediately called a series of meetings consisting of one meeting with the school trustees in the area of each of the proposed consolidated districts.[9] Following these meetings, on February 24 the commission took the following action:

On motion of Commissioner Wilson the clerk was directed to send a copy of the following communication to each of the school trustees in Salt Lake County:

Trustee of Salt Lake County
Dear Sir:
    The Board of County Commissioners having met with the trustees of various school districts in Salt Lake County, and discussed the

[6] A. C. Matheson, in the *Utah Educational Review* of May-June, 1915, states that the first recommendation of Ashton was at the request of the county commissioners. This communication could not be located by the present writer and the commissioners' minutes do not give any help on this point. Matheson's information came from James H. Anderson, one of the commissioners. Ashton had died several years before the article was published. James E. Moss, who was clerk of Granite School District in 1905, when Ashton was superintendent, states that Ashton initiated the plan but before he made the recommendation had to convince the commissioners that they had the power to consolidate.

[7] Biennial State School Report, 1902, *op. cit.*, p. 286.

[8] Matheson states that Ashton at first suggested a consolidation into twelve districts. The writer found no mention of the twelve-district recommendation in the records of the commissioners' meetings. Matheson personally told the writer that he secured his information from talks with Commissioner Anderson.

[9] Minutes of Meetings of Salt Lake County Commission, January 18, 1904 to February 24, 1904.

suggestion of the county superintendent of schools to consolidate certain school districts, call your attention to the following points.

1st. That consolidation of certain districts will be for the improvement of the educational system in this county.

2nd. That the suggestion of the county superintendent is to make eight school districts of the county, while some of the trustees have suggested a more radical step, namely, that the county be consolidated into two school districts, the dividing line to be just south of Murray.

Will you kindly consider these suggestions and inform us specifically, not later than March 19, 1904, which one of the two you regard as preferable.

The record of the vote is shown in the minutes of the meeting of March 21. Of the thirty-six districts and 108 trustees in the county, twenty districts and fifty-one trustees were represented in the vote, which was made by individuals. Two trustees were in favor of eight districts, twenty-three trustees were in favor of two districts, twenty-six trustees did not favor consolidation. Analysis of the vote shows that ten districts favored consolidation. The districts in Murray, Bingham, and East Jordan, all centers of corporate wealth, were opposed to the two-district plan. Sugarhouse and Farmers Ward, two of the more populous districts near Salt Lake City, were also opposed. The commission took no action, and no further record regarding the consolidation question appears in the minutes of its meetings until December.

In the meantime a quiet but active campaign was going on to convert the trustees to the support of consolidation. Members of the county commission and of the state school office, and other interested citizens, together with Superintendent Ashton, met with the local school trustees and small groups of interested citizens in each school district during the summer and fall of 1904.[10] That these meetings received little general publicity is indicated by failure to find a single reference to the meetings or the consolidation question in the Salt Lake City newspapers prior to December.[11] That the campaign was spirited, within its narrow

[10] The oral statements of A. C. Matheson, James E. Moss, Seth Pixton, John W. Smith, Joseph Hibbard, and Lottie Ashton all agree on the general facts of this campaign.

[11] *Deseret Evening News* and *Salt Lake Tribune*, 1904.

circle, is shown by the following statement of Matheson, who was an active campaigner from the state school office:

They [the county commissioners] hoped to convince their fellow citizens that such consolidation would inure to the benefit of all, but found in meetings held for a discussion of the question, that their own views were in direct conflict with prevailing sentiment. They were warned against making such a change and threatened with political extinction at the expiration of their terms of office should they persist in carrying out their avowed intention. They succeeded, however, in winning to their cause one more than half of the 108 school trustees. Thankful for this moral support they continued on their way.[12]

CREATION OF TWO SCHOOL DISTRICTS

On December 10, 1904, Ashton recommended to the commissioners the creation of two school districts in Salt Lake County, outside of Salt Lake City, to be known as the Granite and the Jordan school districts. The reasons given for the recommendation are as follows:

I make this recommendation for the following reasons:
First: This consolidation will equalize the county tax giving to each pupil, regardless of his financial condition, an equal proportion of the said county tax.
Second: It will enable pupils to attend the schools nearest their homes.
Third: It will guarantee high schools, and place them on a basis of proficiency, impossible under the small district conditions.
Fourth: It will place the county schools on a business basis, as the cities of the first and second class are now, by employing skillful accountants to handle the funds, and purchase at the best possible wholesale prices.
Fifth: It will raise the standard of the teachers by making teaching a business requiring the most skillful men and women.
I further recommend that this change go into effect on or prior to January 1, 1905 . . . .[13]

At a meeting on December 15, 1904, the county commissioners accepted the recommendation and passed resolutions creating the two school districts, to become effective July 1, 1905. They also appointed a legislative committee to draft suitable laws for the

[12] Matheson, A. C. "Consolidation of School Districts," *Utah Educational Review,* May-June, 1915, p. 8.
[13] Minutes of Meeting of Salt Lake County Commission, December 15, 1904.

governing of large school districts of this type and to submit these laws to the legislature which was to convene in January, 1905.

Before the motion creating the two school districts was passed, Commissioner Standish offered an amendment to combine the thirty-six local districts into one large district rather than two.

Mr. Standish said, he offered this amendment for the reason that he believed if it was a matter of equalizing taxes among the school districts which was being sought, it would be far better for the purpose to have one district and one board of trustees, but thought the whole matter should be left to the legislature and action should be deferred by this board until such legislature should convene.

Chairman Anderson voted "no" on the amendment, for the reason that under the existing conditions, the consolidating of the entire county into one district would be an impossibility, and that at the present time it would not be as practicable as two districts.

Commissioner Wilson voted "no" on the amendment, for the reason that it was too big a proposition for the Board of County Commissioners to make one district of the whole county, with only a board of three trustees.

Standish voted for the original resolutions because he thought that the unanimous vote of the commissioners would carry more weight with the legislature than if the commissioners were divided.

It is probable that the effective date of organization was deferred to July 1, 1905 in order to permit the new districts from the beginning to have any advantages which legislative action might secure for them. Provision was made in the resolutions for the county attorney to provide legal forms for the conveyance of all property from the old districts to the new, but no definite mention appears about the bonded indebtedness of the districts. John W. Smith, newly elected county superintendent of schools in the 1904 elections, stated that it was generally assumed that the larger district would assume all the obligations of the smaller ones and that he so advised some districts that were building schoolhouses prior to July 1, 1905. The law, as later passed by the legislature, required the consolidated district to assume all obligations of the smaller districts.

The two new districts together had a school population of 9,148 in July, 1905. Many of these children were soon lost to the county system by the incorporation of Murray as a second class city and the extension of the boundaries of Salt Lake City. Jordan district, in July, 1907, had a school population of 3,969 and Granite district's school population was 4,411.

When the districts were organized in 1905, B. W. Ashton was appointed superintendent of schools in Granite district and John W. Smith, although theoretically holding the office of county superintendent of schools, was chosen as the superintendent of the Jordan district.

REASONS FOR TWO DISTRICTS IN SALT LAKE COUNTY

When Commissioner Standish attempted to have the county consolidated into one school district, the other commissioners voted against the motion because they thought the formation of the larger district would be impractical or impossible. One reason for this attitude may have been the distances of travel necessary in supervision and control of such a large district. It was about twenty-five miles from one end of the county to the other, the usual mode of transportation at that time was the horse-drawn carriage, and there was no precedent in Utah to show how well a large, consolidated, rural school district could be organized and administered.

It is doubtful if the factor of pupil transportation affected the final decision as to the size of the unit for school administration in Salt Lake County. When Superintendent Ashton recommended the creation of eight districts in the county, he doubtless intended to have only one high school in each school district. When the commissioners decided to create only two school districts in the county it seems to have been taken for granted that more than one high school would be required in each consolidated district.[14] Each district within a few years of its organization established more than one high school. The decision to create two school districts instead of eight, as first suggested, involved an assumption that the size of the attendance unit and the size of the administration unit were separate factors.

[14] Minutes of Meeting of the Salt Lake County Commission, December 15, 1904.

Another consideration was the possibility that the district board of education would consist of only three men and that this number could not adequately represent various sections of a large territory. Until the legislature acted on the proposed law the new school districts must be organized under the older school law providing for a board of three trustees.

However, a major factor that probably contributed to the formation of two districts was the division of Salt Lake County, outside of Salt Lake City, into two sections for the administration of the affairs of the dominant church. Each of these large divisions, called "stakes," were subdivided into local congregations called "wards." The two church stakes in rural Salt Lake County in 1904 covered the same territory and bore the same names as the two school districts that were created.[15] The existence of a church organization for each of these two sections of the county very probably was a conditioning factor in the decision to form two school districts.

POPULAR OPINION AND CONSOLIDATION

Considering the various factors in the situation, it is probable that leaders in education, government, and business were in general in favor of consolidation but that the proposition to consolidate the schools would probably have been defeated in a popular vote. The districts in Murray were bitterly opposed to consolidation and this is one factor that contributed to the incorporation of Murray as a second class city in June, 1905, thus making it an independent school district.[16] Since the commissioners did not consolidate the county districts until after the November elections in 1904, it is probable that they did not wish to make an issue of consolidation at the polls at that time. Pertinent to this situation also is the fact that the people had defeated the earlier attempt to consolidate for high school purposes only. Of fourteen people who had taken an active part in the process of consolidation in Salt Lake County, and who were interviewed by the

[15] Information checked in Historian's Office, Church of Jesus Christ of Latter Day Saints, Salt Lake City, Utah.

[16] *Report of the County Superintendent of District Schools of Salt Lake County, Utah,* July 1, 1907, p. 39.

writer, few would say that they thought the people would have voted favorably for consolidation, and at least a majority were confident that such a proposal would have been defeated if referred to popular vote.

On the other hand, much support from influential sources came to the men who were working for consolidation. For instance, on December 15, 1904, the morning of the day the county commissioners voted to consolidate, the *Salt Lake Tribune* in an editorial voiced approval of the plan. In part, the editorial stated:

> The effort of County School Superintendent Ashton to consolidate the school districts of this county outside of the city into two districts, is a work in the right direction. The prime result of such consolidation would be the strengthening of the [elementary school] classes and the establishment of high schools, both of which are needs of the time, and would be of much advantage to the pupils and to the cause of education.

> .   .   .   .   .   .

> There is no doubt of the merit of the plan and we trust that the superintendent may be aided in carrying his plan to the complete success that it merits.[17]

This paper, which represented important mining and financial interests of the state, had explained the plan in the issue of the previous day, and in the December 15 issue printed an interview with State Superintendent A. C. Nelson, quoting him as enthusiastically supporting Mr. Ashton's efforts to consolidate Salt Lake County schools.

One cannot be positive that the people would not have voted for consolidation, but it is obvious that the method used to win support for consolidation was to work with representatives of the people rather than with the mass. There is no record of the county commissioners trying to secure a vote of anyone other than the school trustees.

COUNTY SCHOOL DISTRICT LAW OF 1905

Under the existing school law, each of the two large school districts which had been created in Salt Lake County would be administered by a board of three members which would not have

[17] *Salt Lake Tribune,* December 15, 1904.

authority to appoint a superintendent of schools or other officers necessary for the administration of a large school system, and which would lack other important powers for efficient conduct of the schools, such as that of borrowing money.

The committee appointed by the county commission to draft appropriate legislation and work for its enactment into law had a bill introduced into the legislature on January 26. It was entitled:

An Act Providing for County School Districts of the First Class, Placing Them upon the Same Basis of Administration as School Districts in Cities of the Second Class, and Making Necessary Regulations Therefor[18]

At the time the bill was introduced the newspapers commented favorably about it, the *Deseret Evening News* stating that it would doubtless be enacted into law and the *Salt Lake Tribune* praising the optional feature of the proposed law.[19] The house passed the measure on March 8 by a vote of thirty-seven ayes and six nays, and the senate passed it on March 9 without a dissenting vote.

As finally enacted into law, the bill had certain features that are pertinent to a study of the process of the adoption of the county-unit system in Utah. These features are as follows:

1. Any school district, existing or that should be created, that had a school population of 3,000 or more was to become a county school district of the first class and to be governed by the new law. The bill did not alter the power of county commissioners to consolidate school districts. The legislature, therefore, approved the practice of leaving the creation of county school districts of the first class to the discretion of the commissioners in each county. However, by placing the size of the school districts at 3,000 school population, the legislature limited the application of the law in 1905 to six counties other than Salt Lake County. These were the counties of Boxelder, Cache, Sanpete, Sevier, Utah, and Weber.[20]

---

[18] *House Journal of the Sixth Session of the Legislature of the State of Utah,* 1905, p. 820.

[19] *Deseret Evening News,* January 26, 1905, and *Salt Lake Tribune,* January 27, 1905.

[20] *Sixth Report of the Superintendent of Public Instruction of the State of Utah,* 1906, Statistical Section, p. 1.

2. The general provision in the new law, placing the county school districts of the first class on the same basis of administration as school districts in cities of the second class, indicates that the experience of the state with these city school districts had been satisfactory and shows that the general pattern of the administrative setup for the new districts was based upon experience within the state.

3. The designation of a board of education of five members to be elected from representative districts at elections held at a separate time from political elections was also based upon experience with the second class cities.

ALL COUNTIES NOT INCLUDED IN LAW

As originally introduced into the legislature, the bill would have permitted any county to become a school district of the first class if it desired. The official house journal does not give the contents of the bills introduced, but the *Deseret Evening News* quotes a passage of the original bill, as follows:

Among the many provisions of the bill, which seeks to grant unto all counties of the state, the privileges to be taken advantage of by Salt Lake County, now consolidated into one [*sic*] county school district, is the following:

Whenever the board of county commissioners of any county shall organize or consolidate the whole county, outside of cities of the first and second classes, into one district, the said district shall be regarded as a county school district of the first class, irrespective of the number of school children in said district, and governed by the provisions of this act relating to county school districts of the first class.[21]

The 3,000 school population minimum was also included in the bill in order to legalize the division of Salt Lake County into two districts.

When the bill came up for passage in the house of representatives, Representative Joseph of Salt Lake City made strenuous efforts to strike out the county clause, but the effort failed and the bill went to the senate containing both the county clause and the 3,000 population clause.[22] The bill was reported out of the

[21] *Deseret Evening News,* January 26, 1905.
[22] *Ibid.,* March 8, 1905.

senate education committee "with minor amendments."[23] Upon
the return of the bill to the house, Representative Joseph and
several other representatives who had voted against the bill when
it first passed the house, now voted for its adoption. It seems
evident that the county-unit feature of the bill had been deleted
in the senate committee, through the influence of forces which
did not wish to see some of the smaller counties consolidated
into a single unit.

SUMMARY

The thirty-six school districts which served approximately
25,000 people in rural Salt Lake County in 1904 had remained
practically unchanged since 1883, thus contributing to maladjustment between the schools and the needs of the growing population.
Although high school facilities were greatly needed, an attempt
to establish a county high school district, in 1903, was defeated
by popular vote.

The county superintendent of schools recommended to the
county commission, in 1904, that it consolidate thirty-six school
districts into eight, but the suggestion was made to the commissioners in meetings with the trustees that two districts, instead
of eight, should be created. The commissioners found that a majority of the trustees were not in favor of consolidation when it
was first proposed. After an eight months' campaign with the
trustees, a majority declared themselves in favor of it and the
thirty-six districts were consolidated into two districts, Granite
and Jordan.

In 1905 a law was passed by the legislature giving the new
districts the same general powers and form of organization as
the school districts in second class cities. In order to become a
county school district of the first class a district must have a
school population of at least 3,000. In 1905 there were at least
3,000 school children in each of six counties other than Salt Lake
County, making it possible for the county commissioners of these
counties to consolidate their school districts into county school

[23] *Senate Journal of the Sixth Session of the Legislature of the State of Utah,*
1905, p. 391.

districts of the first class, if, and when, the commissioners thought such consolidation desirable.

ANALYTICAL SUMMARY STATEMENTS

In analyzing the process of the development of the county-unit plan, as related to the first adoption and the enactment of the permissive law, the following statements are pertinent to the understanding of the process of adaptation.

1. If the attempt to form a county high school district in Salt Lake County in 1903 had been successful, a dual rather than a unitary system of public school organization in each county might have been formed in Utah.

2. The first known recommendation in Utah of a county school superintendent to the county commission for consolidation of school districts on a large scale resulted in a series of meetings with representatives of the public, in which the suggestions were expanded and the plan made more effective. At the time the two-district plan was adopted considerable sentiment had developed for a one-district system.

3. The limitation of the right to establish county school districts of the first class to districts having at least 3,000 school children limited the opportunity of diffusion of the county-unit plan to counties of comparatively large population.

4. The enactment of the school law of 1905 did not give any assistance to the majority of the counties of the state in the solution of the high school problem.

CHAPTER IV

DIFFUSION OF THE COUNTY-UNIT PLAN

DURING the ten-year period following the enactment of the county-unit law of 1905, fifteen Utah counties, exclusive of Salt Lake County, became eligible to consolidate their school districts under the new plan. This chapter briefly explains the actions of these counties regarding consolidation of their school districts under the new law; the changes made in the school laws prior to 1915 which affected the consolidation problem; and the enactment of the mandatory law of 1915 which completely diffused the county-unit organization throughout the state.

Certain data relating to the county-unit plan in the sixteen counties eligible to adopt it prior to 1915 are contained in Table I. The location of these various counties in the state is shown in Map I. An examination of the data in Table I shows that eight counties consolidated their school districts prior to 1915 and that four other counties officially considered the problem. In general, explanation of the action taken by each county will be given in chronological order.

COUNTY CONSOLIDATION

Weber County. Of the six Utah counties other than Salt Lake County that were eligible in 1905 to organize county school districts of the first class, Weber was the first to take advantage of the new law. There is evidence that many school and civic leaders in Weber County had been favorable to county consolidation of schools prior to 1905. The county superintendent's reports of 1902 and 1904 contain recommendations for the creation of county school districts. Also, early in January, 1903 the problem of county consolidation was discussed at a meeting of school district trustees and teachers held in offices of the Weber County commissioners in Ogden and a special committee was appointed

TABLE I

DATA RELATING TO ACTION ON CONSOLIDATION OF SCHOOLS
IN SIXTEEN UTAH COUNTIES, 1905 TO 1914, INCLUSIVE

County	Date Eligible to Consolidate	School Population at Date of Eligibility	Date Consolidation First Considered by Commission	Date Consolidation Became Effective	Number of Districts Organized
Salt Lake ..	1905	9,148	Feb., 1904	July, 1905	2
Weber	1905	3,259	June, 1905	July, 1905	1
Boxelder ...	1905	3,876	May, 1907	July, 1907	1
Cache	1905	4,747	Feb., 1908	Mar., 1908	1
Morgan	1908[a]	725	Apr., 1907	Nov., 1908	1
Davis	1907	3,017	May, 1907	July, 1911	1
Sevier	1905	3,045	Feb., 1908	Feb., 1912	1
Uintah	1913	2,598	Feb., 1914	Mar., 1914	1
Sanpete	1905	4,953	Sept., 1906		(2)[b]
Summit	1911	2,513	Aug., 1910		(3)
Millard	1913	2,427	Mar., 1913		(1)
Carbon	1913	2,494	Dec., 1913		(1)
Utah	1905	8,738			(2)
Juab	1909	3,125			(2)
Wasatch ...	1910	3,039			(2)[c]
Tooele	1913	2,076			(1)

[a] For eligibility of this county, see p. 51.

[b] Numbers in parentheses indicate high school districts organized in 1911.

[c] One of these two districts became Duchesne County district in 1915.

to draft a plan for consolidation.[1] Although no further action
appears to have resulted from this meeting, it is evident that
school and county officials had considered the problem prior to
1905 and that the introduction of the county-unit law into the
legislature at that time found many Weber County leaders favorable to its provisions.

During the time the measure was before the legislature, members of that body from Weber County asked the county superintendent of schools, W. N. Petterson, to spend a few days in Salt
Lake City and work for the passage of the bill in the legislature.
This Petterson did. After the legislature adjourned, some individual conferences were held with the county commissioners of
Weber County which resulted in the tentative approval, by two
of the three commissioners, of the county-unit plan.

[1] *Deseret Evening News*, January 12, 1903, p. 7.

A petition, signed by Petterson and some interested school trustees and teachers, requesting the consolidation of the twenty-

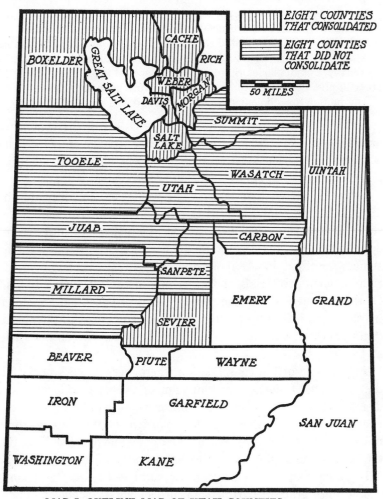

MAP I. OUTLINE MAP OF UTAH COUNTIES 1905-1914

four rural school districts of the county into one school district, was considered by the county commissioners on June 19, 1905. Chairman Joseph Stanford read a resolution approving the plan and moved that a committee be appointed to prepare appropriate resolutions.

Opposition to the motion was made as described in the following quoted paragraph:

Commissioner Wilson stated he understood that the majority of the residents of Weber County outside of Ogden City were opposed to the consolidation of the school districts, and if the board contemplated making such action he would move as an amendment to the motion offered by Commissioner Stanford that a special election be called in order to give the people an opportunity to vote upon the matter. The motion amendment received no second and was lost.[2]

Stanford and Petterson presented the report of the committee on July 3, 1905, at which time the Weber County school district was created, to become effective immediately, all resolutions being passed by a vote of two in favor and one opposed.

Petterson stated that no attempt was made to ascertain the attitude of the public toward the consolidation.[3] He stated that some antagonism developed, but it did not grow into serious opposition. The investigator found news reports of the commissioners' meetings in the newspaper of general circulation in the county but no editorials and no letters of protest from citizens.[4] Of the five members of the county board of education appointed by the commissioners in July, four were continued in their position by popular vote at the school board elections which were held in December.

At the time of the consolidation, there were 3,259 school children in Weber County, distributed among twenty-four local school districts, the largest of which contained 346 children. Some districts maintaining a nine months' school had a tax rate of three mills on each dollar of assessed valuation, while one district maintaining a seven months' school had a tax rate of fifteen mills.[5] The only public high school work in the rural sections of the county was a ninth grade department in an elementary school building, in which ten ninth grade pupils were enrolled. Within a few miles of the rural districts was the city of Ogden which maintained

[2] Minutes of Meeting of Weber County Commission, June 19, 1905, Ogden.
[3] Personal interviews.
[4] *Ogden Standard,* Ogden, Utah, June 1 to August 15, 1905.
[5] Special report in Minutes of the Meeting of the Weber County Commission, July 3, 1905.

high grade elementary and high school education for its children. It is evident that the people of rural Weber County were willing to support a school system that would give their children better educational opportunities.

School Law Amendments in 1907. In 1907 two ambiguities in the 1905 law were removed by the legislature. An amendment was made to the high school law definitely stating that a county school district of the first class was also a high school district and had a right to levy a separate high school tax. Because the amended law of 1905 did not clearly give authority to a school district, having at least 3,000 children, to become a county school district of the first class, if it was the only school district in the county, the following clause was added to the first section of the law:

Provided, where an entire county is constituted into one school district it shall be a county school district of the first class.[6]

Although this amendment might appear to have extended the right to create a county school district of the first class to any county in the state, regardless of population, rulings of the attorney general and interpretations of the state school department seem to assume that the 3,000 school population clause was a requirement for eligibility to consolidate.

Boxelder County. The consolidation of schools in Boxelder County was in several ways similar to the procedures followed in Weber County. One of the men who first recommended it had served in the 1905 session of the legislature, the question of consolidation was before the commission only a short time, and no attempt was made to determine the attitude of the voters toward it.

On May 20, 1907, F. W. Fishburn of Brigham City, a representative of Boxelder County in the state legislature, presented a petition to the county commission asking that the school districts of Boxelder County be united into a county school district of the first class. Although several petitions were presented to the commissioners protesting the consolidation, they voted unan-

[6] *Laws of the State of Utah Passed at the Seventh Regular Session of the Legislature of the State of Utah,* 1907, p. 142.

imously on June 17, 1907, to create the Boxelder County school district.[7]

During the brief period that the problem was being considered by the county commissioners, consolidation was receiving the enthusiastic support of the local newspaper, and before the final decision to consolidate was made by the commission, Fishburn's petition had received the approval of the Brigham City Commercial Club.[8]

The interest of non-residents in the consolidation problem of a county is shown in the case of Boxelder. Two of the petitions against consolidation were presented by non-resident taxpayers. In favor of consolidation, Mathonihah Thomas, of Salt Lake City, was present at two meetings of the county commission. Thomas, who was an attorney and a member of the Salt Lake City board of education, had worked for consolidation in rural Salt Lake County, and was now assisting in extending the county-unit plan to other counties of the state.

Cache County. The consolidation of the school districts of Cache County was marked by bitter opposition at the time of consolidation and for some time thereafter. This was probably due to a peculiar combination of circumstances which created misunderstanding between the county commissioners and a large number of citizens.

On February 8, 1908, at an institute of Cache County teachers held in Logan, speakers from Salt Lake County explained the advantages of consolidation. A resolution was passed at the meeting asking County Superintendent J. L. McCarrey to request the county commissioners to call a mass meeting of citizens to discuss the question of consolidating the school districts of Cache County, outside of Logan City. The county commission published notices for such a meeting to be held in Logan on February 29.

Inquiries of citizens came to the local paper asking if a vote on the question would be held.[9] The editor stated that an election would not be held on the question because there was no authority

[7] Minutes of Meetings of Boxelder County Commission, May-June, 1907.

[8] *Boxelder News,* Brigham City, Utah, May 30, 1907 and June 20, 1907.

[9] *The Journal,* Logan, Utah, February 11, 1908.

in the law for placing it before the people in that way. The statement concluded:

If it will result in a betterment of our schools in general and provide us with high schools in this county, as it has done elsewhere, narrow local prejudices and objections to petty details should not be allowed to prevent its adoption. But even a good thing should not be forced upon a majority of the people, for the will of the majority should obtain, and it likely will, at least that is the purpose of the commissioners in calling the meeting referred to.

This statement probably gave the impression that the commissioners had promised to abide by the will of the people as expressed in the mass meeting, but the commission later denied this in a public statement, pointing out that they had called the meeting at the request of the county superintendent of schools, that he had arranged the program, and that the commissioners had attended only as interested spectators.[10] However, published notices of the meeting were authorized by the commission.

A majority of those present at the meeting on February 29 were opposed to consolidation. Part of the report of the meeting by the local newspaper is illuminating:

A general discussion followed but it revealed nothing more than this: those precincts that have a good thing in a school may want to hold on to it and those that have not, desire a more equitable distribution of the county property between the districts. Human selfishness stood out more boldly than anything else, and the discussion, therefore, was of little value to the commissioners, who are face to face with the question of what should be done for the benefit of all the schools of the county, rather than for the benefit of one or a few.[11]

On March 7 the county commissioners issued a public statement giving figures of school population and per capita assessed valuations in the twenty-five school districts of the county, showing that a five mill tax would yield revenue of $3.23 per child in the poorest district and $43.78 per child in the richest one. They frankly stated in conclusion that they considered these conditions unjust to the taxpayers and school children of the county and that they intended to remedy such conditions, either through county

10 Minutes of Meeting of Cache County Commission, May 15, 1908.
11 *The Journal*, Logan, Utah, March 3, 1908.

consolidation or by changing the boundaries of the school districts of the county.[12]

On March 23 the county commission, by a unanimous vote, consolidated the school districts of the county into a county school district of the first class.

Under the impression that the commissioners had repudiated a promise to abide by the will of the people, many citizens of the county protested the act of consolidation. Meetings of protest were held at which anti-consolidation committees were organized, and the commissioners were threatened with political extinction if they did not disorganize the district they had created. Although they showed no signs of desiring to reconsider their action, the commissioners were advised, by both the county and the state attorneys, that they had no authority to dissolve a county school district of the first class after it had been created.[13]

The opposition did everything in its power to undo the acts of the commission. A suit was instituted in the district court to force disorganization of the district, but it was finally withdrawn without decision. Two anti-consolidationists ran for the office of county commissioners in the political elections of November, 1908, but only one was elected, thus leaving a majority of the commission in favor of consolidation. In December, 1908, when school board elections were held, all the members of the board who ran for election were defeated, thus placing an entirely new board in authority.[14] But the new board of education firmly carried forward the work of the county school district. Not until April 1, 1911, when a school bond issue was carried by the people, could one say that organized opposition to the act of consolidation had ceased.[15]

It is probable that the opposition to consolidation in Cache County would have been no greater, and no more enduring, than the opposition in Weber and Boxelder Counties had been, if the misunderstanding between the commissioners and the people had

---

[12] *The Journal,* Logan, Utah, March 7, 1908.

[13] *Seventh Report of the Superintendent of Public Instruction of the State of Utah,* 1908, p. 404.

[14] Minutes of Meeting of Cache County Board of Education, December 7, 1908.

[15] *Ibid.,* April 1, 1911.

not arisen over the calling of the mass meeting of citizens in February, 1908.

Morgan County. In 1907 there were 726 school children in Morgan County, too few to permit the county to be organized as a county school district of the first class. An inquiry to the attorney general as to the status of special funds of the thirteen school districts, in the event of consolidation, was answered on the basis of the law applying to local school districts.[16] Presumably, then, consolidation of schools, if effected in this county, would be legalized under the local district school laws rather than according to the new law for first class districts.

County Superintendent of Schools Rachel C. Farley first recommended consolidation of the school districts of the county to the county commissioners in April, 1907. The problem was discussed at meetings of the commission at various times during the next year but no action was taken until September 21, 1908, when the commissioners decided to submit the consolidation question to a vote of the people at the regular political election in November. The vote was favorable and on November 10, 1908, the Morgan County school district was created. The commission then organized the district as a county school district of the first class, appointing five members of the board of education, each from a representative district of the county, and the board assumed all the powers which the law gave to the county-unit district.[17] No record was found of any legal authority for this action or of any protest ever being made against it.

Although the state superintendent of schools, in each biennial report from 1906 to 1914, urged the legislature to amend the law to make it possible for any county to create a county school district of the first class, irrespective of its population, and the legislature responded by reducing the population requirements in 1911 and in 1913, after 1908 Morgan County appears to have been the proof that a small county could so organize without waiting for revised legislation.

The reason for the popular vote being favorable to consolida-

[16] Biennial State School Report, 1908, *op. cit.*, p. 397.
[17] Minutes of Meeting of Morgan County Commission, November 10, 1908.

tion in Morgan County was probably twofold. Although the town of Morgan, the only incorporated area in the county, and the county seat, had less than a thousand inhabitants, it was divided into two school districts. In 1908 there was no high school education offered in the county.[18] The people probably wished to have a district large enough to maintain a high school. The town of Morgan was neither large enough nor wealthy enough to do this, since the corporate wealth of the county (a railroad line and a large cement plant) was outside of the town. The records of the commissioners' meetings make it evident that the desire to have the corporate wealth of the county do more to help support the schools in the towns was one of the deciding factors in the election.

Changes in School Law in 1911 and 1913. In 1911 the legislature repealed the existing high school laws and adopted a new high school code. The people had recently approved a constitutional amendment authorizing a state tax of one-half mill for state aid to high schools. In order to assure the establishing of high schools in all parts of the state, the legislature now required each county that was not organized into one or more county school districts of the first class to organize a county high school district, with a board of education consisting of the county superintendent of schools and one member from each of the local school boards within the high school district. The law permitted a county to be divided into two or more high school districts by the board of county commissioners. This section tacitly recognized the fact that certain counties in the state were divided into separate regions by topography and industrial conditions which made it advisable to permit the organization of more than one consolidated school district in each of these counties.[19]

The new high school districts were given authority to levy a tax of five mills for high school purposes. The repeal of the old high school laws inadvertently took authority away from the county school districts of the first class to levy a special tax for

---

[18] Biennial State School Report, 1908, *op. cit.*, Statistical Tables.
[19] *Laws of the State of Utah passed at the Ninth Regular Session of the Legislature of the State of Utah,* 1911, pp. 14, 47, and 267.

high schools and placed some of these districts under a financial handicap until the error was corrected by the 1913 legislature.[20]

The law governing the county school districts of the first class was also amended in 1911 to lower the population requirement to 2,500. In 1913 the requirement was changed to 2,000. During the same sessions at which it liberalized the population requirements for county school districts, the legislature added certain restrictions to the process of consolidation. In 1911 a clause was inserted into the law which probably was intended to require the consent of one third of the taxpayers of a county before consolidation could take place, but it was so poorly phrased that it was ineffective. In 1913 a direct requirement was included in the law that a majority of the voters in a county must approve consolidation before the county commission could put it into effect.[21] This law took a discretionary power from the county commission that it had been given when the territory was first organized.

Davis County. The enactment of the high school law of 1911 had the immediate effect of influencing favorable action on consolidation of the school districts in Davis and Sevier Counties.

The first recommendation that a county school district be created in Davis County was made to the county commission by Superintendent Whitesides in May, 1907, the first year that Davis County had sufficient school population to be eligible to consolidate. The recommendation was considered at several meetings, and in June action was postponed until the following year. At a meeting of the commission held March 16, 1908, the recommendation of the county superintendent was again considered and tabled indefinitely. During the year preceding this action, the question had been thoroughly discussed in the county, protests or petitions from practically all local school districts had been presented to the commission, and the commission decided that the people were not in favor of organizing a county unit.

Throughout the discussion of consolidation in 1907 and 1908, when the problem was being considered by the commissioners,

[20] Biennial State School Report, 1912, *op. cit.*, p. 22.
[21] *Laws of the State of Utah passed at the Tenth Regular Session of the Legislature of the State of Utah,* 1913, p. 184 ff.

the principal arguments for and against consolidation centered around the desirability of high schools which, it was admitted, would be more easily established under consolidation. Early newspaper comments in 1907 questioned the value of high school education. At a meeting of school trustees held at Farmington on February 25, 1908, President Kingsbury of the University of Utah urged the need for high schools in Davis County. The editor of a local paper summed up the report of the meeting as follows:

> The matter resolves itself into the fact whether or not we are in favor of high schools, if so, it would seem that consolidation is the best, otherwise it would be better not.[22]

It is probable that the decision of the commissioners in 1907 and 1908 not to consolidate reflected an attitude on the part of many people in Davis County at that time, that the establishing of free tax-supported high schools was not desirable.

After the passage of the high school district law in 1911, which forced the establishment of at least one high school in each county, County Superintendent Burton met with the commission on May 15 and recommended the creation of one high school district in Davis County. The question of consolidation for all purposes came before the meeting and the commission voted to call a mass meeting of citizens to be held at Farmington on June 22, 1911, to consider the problem.

Eleven of the thirteen school districts of the county were represented at this meeting. After considerable discussion of all phases of the problem, including the necessary consolidation for high school purposes, a motion to ask the county commission to consolidate the district schools was voted upon, six districts voting in favor and five districts either voting no or reporting a divided vote. A majority of individuals present were favorable to consolidation. A committee, of which Henry H. Blood was chairman, was appointed to present the decision to the county commission.[23] Mr. Blood made his report on July 3 and on that day the commissioners created the Davis County school district.

---

[22] *Davis County Clipper*, Kaysville, Utah, February 21, 1908, p. 1. See also issue of May 31, 1907, p. 5, for article questioning the value of high school education.

[23] Minutes of Meeting of Davis County Commission, July 3, 1911.

Sevier County. County Superintendent P. D. Jensen recommended the consolidation of the school districts of Sevier County on February 3, 1908. The county commission invited trustees of local school districts to send delegates to a meeting on April 7, at Richfield, to discuss the problem. At this meeting fifteen of the sixteen local school districts were represented by delegates who, in most instances, had been elected at mass meetings of citizens in the local districts. Although nine of the fifteen districts were in favor of consolidation, they were, in general, the smaller districts.[24] The delegation from Richfield, the largest town in the county, was evenly divided on the question. Salina, the largest district in the north end of the county, was almost unanimously opposed to consolidation at this time. Both Richfield and Salina were maintaining graded elementary schools and high schools. No decision was made at the meeting of April 7, and two months later the commission decided, by a two-to-one vote, to postpone action indefinitely.

The legislature of 1911 passed the high school district law while the Sevier County commissioners were holding a series of meetings with district school trustees for the purpose of more nearly equalizing the property valuations among the several districts. After brief consideration of the new high school law the commission published notice for any district to show cause by July 1, 1911, why the districts should not be consolidated for all purposes.[25] One of the districts that had been in favor of consolidation in 1908 now requested delay. The request was granted. In October the commissioners appointed a committee of five to determine if one third or more of the taxpayers of the county desired consolidation. The signatures of that number were secured by the committee and the Sevier County school district was established on February 6, 1912.

The commissioners gave two reasons for the consolidation, one of which was a desire to equalize the county tax and educational opportunity. The other reason was to avoid the creation of the county high school district. According to the provisions of that

---

[24] Minutes of Meeting of Sevier County Commission, April 7, 1908.
[25] *Ibid.,* May 2, 1911.

law, the high school board of education in Sevier County would consist of seventeen members, most of whom would represent small communities. The commissioners became convinced in the discussion prior to 1912 that, if the county high school district were organized, attempts would be made to establish too many small high schools. This danger could be partially avoided by the creation of a county board of education with five members.[26]

Uintah County. In 1913, the first year that the school population of Uintah County was large enough to permit creation of a county school district of the first class, the following news item appeared in the *Utah Educational Review*:

> As a result of the recent visit of State Superintendent A. C. Nelson and his corps of institute workers, the consolidation of the public school districts of Uintah County has taken form and will likely carry with very little opposition. The county superintendent, Mr. N. G. Sowards, and one member of each board of trustees have held an executive session to formulate a plan for accomplishing this consolidation.[27]

On February 2, 1914, Sowards made the formal recommendation to the commission that the school districts be consolidated. Petitions were circulated and signed by a majority of the voters in the county and on March 2, 1914, the Uintah school district was created as a county school district of the first class.[28] Mr. W. H. Siddoway, a member of the county commission in 1914, states that one of the principal reasons for the consolidation was the desire to secure equalization of the property tax, the inequalities of which had been emphasized by the practice of many owners of property in the rural areas of the county who moved their families into Vernal during the winter in order to secure the benefits of good schools. An equalized county tax would require all property of the county to contribute equally to the schooling of children wherever they might be in attendance.

COUNTIES NOT FAVORABLE TO CONSOLIDATION

Of the sixteen counties eligible at some time prior to 1915 to create county school districts of the first class, eight did not con-

[26] Explanation confirmed in interviews with Sevier County residents.
[27] *Utah Educational Review*, Vol. 7, No. 4, December, 1913, p. 26.
[28] Minutes of Meetings of Uintah County Commission, February and March, 1914.

solidate their schools. In three of these counties the problem was seriously considered and decisions were made not to consolidate. In one county the question was under consideration in 1915 when the mandatory law was passed, and in four counties the question appears never to have officially come before the county commissioners for decision.

Utah County. At the time the permissive county school district law was passed in 1905, Utah County, exclusive of Provo City, had 8,738 school children, more than any other county except Salt Lake. It might be expected that this county would be one of the first to consider the consolidation of its school districts under the new law, but such was not the case. Examination of the minutes of meetings of the Utah County commission fails to show a single instance in which the county superintendent of schools or a group of citizens petitioned the commission to consolidate the schools into a county school district of the first class. There is evidence that the consolidation problem was considered by special committees of citizens,[29] but J. Preston Creer, who was county superintendent of schools for several years after 1911, states that a formal recommendation was not made to the commission because it was known that the county-unit plan could not be effected in Utah County. In May, 1911, after the passage of the high school district law by the legislature, Superintendent Creer recommended the creation of two high school districts, which recommendation was carried into effect. There is no record of any discussion at that time of the desirability of consolidating for all purposes.

Two reasons for the apparent lack of interest in consolidation in Utah County may be suggested. One of these is related to the geography of the populated area of the county and the other concerns the presence of a large number of incorporated towns that are well distributed throughout the populated area. The populated section of the county is in the shape of a crescent about forty miles in length, with the open part to the west bordering on Utah Lake. On the north, east, and south the valley is en-

---

[29] Monahan, A. C. *County-Unit Organization for the Administration of Rural Schools*, p. 51. Bulletin No. 44, U. S. Bureau of Education, 1914.

closed by mountains. Almost in the middle of this half circle is the second class city of Provo, extending from the mountains on the east to the lake on the west and cutting the rural section of the county into two separate parts. This division of the county into two distinct parts would tend to encourage the formation of two separate districts in the event of consolidation, as illustrated by the creation of two high school districts in 1911.

Another factor affecting the problem in Utah County was the presence of three incorporated towns, or third class cities, in each of the two sections of the county. Each of these towns had one school district for a population of not less than 2,500. All of the towns were offering high school work in 1905, and they were located in such a way that a high school was accessible, within a few miles, to most of the residents of the county. These conditions of geography, as well as the size of incorporated towns, probably made consolidation of school districts appear to the public representatives of the people of Utah County not to be so desirable as it was in many other counties of the state.

Sanpete County. Having a school population of nearly 5,000, Sanpete County was eligible to consolidate its schools in 1905. The first recommendation to create a county school district was made by Superintendent Larsen on September 4, 1906. The request was denied by the county commission at that time. The question was revived in 1908 and was again denied. In 1909 a petition was again presented to the commission and committees from various school districts met with the commissioners. The general attitude of the people appeared to be against consolidation and the commission again refused to consolidate.

During the period from 1906 to 1909, opposition to consolidation appears to have centered in the southern part of the county, especially in the towns of Manti and Ephraim. The Manti Commercial Club, after a series of meetings on the problem, voted unanimously to oppose it. A meeting of district school trustees of the county, held in Ephraim on August 26, voted against consolidation by a majority of seven to one. The principal objections to consolidation appear to have arisen from fear that a county board of education would interfere with the local building program and the school work for which the buildings were designed.[30]

After the passage of the high school law in 1911, the county superintendent of schools recommended the consolidation of the county into either one or two county school districts of the first class rather than the creation of separate high school districts. At this time meetings were held with representatives of all districts and the question was thoroughly discussed, but on February 6, 1912 the commission voted to leave the local school districts as they were because they thought that consolidation could not be successful under the existing law.[31] Two high school districts were then created.

Interviews with residents of Sanpete County gave information that the commissioners would have consolidated the schools in 1912 if the law had not limited the tax rate for county school districts of the first class to such an extent that Sanpete County could not maintain its schools if it consolidated. This point of view agrees with data presented by the state superintendent, which show that between 1911 and 1913, in so far as ability to raise revenue was concerned, counties were actually penalized by creating county school districts of the first class.[32]

Juab County. Although Juab County had sufficient school children in 1909 to consolidate as a county school district of the first class, the populated area of the county was divided into two widely separated sections, one a mining center and the other an agricultural area. Mountains and poor roads separated these areas and no attempt was made to unite them into one school district. In 1911 two high school districts were created, one for each section of the county.

Wasatch County. Although Wasatch County theoretically had more than 3,000 school children in 1910, part of these were located in the eastern section of the county which was separated from the western part by more than fifty miles of mountainous country, the roads of which were impassable during the greater

[30] *Manti Messenger,* Manti, Utah, August 26 and September 12, 1909.
[31] Minutes of Meeting of Sanpete County Commission, February 5, 1912.
[32] Biennial State School Report, 1912, *op. cit.,* p. 22.

part of the school year. In 1911 two separate high school districts were created, and in January, 1915 the eastern section was organized into a separate county, Duchesne. Creation of county school districts of the first class does not appear to have been considered by the county commission prior to 1915.

Summit County. The populated area of Summit County is divided into three distinct sections by mountain ranges. Two areas are located in river valleys and one is a mining region on a mountainside. In 1910, when a redistricting of local school districts was under way for the purpose of more nearly equalizing property valuations between local school units, the county superintendent recommended consolidation into one school district, but the county commissioners thought it impractical and refused to give the question serious consideration.[33] After the passage of the high school law in 1911, the county was divided into three high school districts.

Millard County. For many years prior to 1913 the county commission of Millard County was repeatedly being petitioned by the newer settlements for a redivision of the railroad property in the county which had been divided between the older settlements by extension of their school district boundaries, and which they refused to share with the more recently settled communities.[34] In 1911 a county high school district had been organized and in March, 1913 the county became eligible to organize as a county school district of the first class. County Superintendent Ashman recommended the consolidation, and it was at once discussed throughout the county. In August, 1913, petitions favorable to consolidation, signed by 1,200 people, were presented to the commission. Because of intense feelings of rival groups, the commissioners postponed action for two months. During this time meetings were held in various parts of the county and a bitter fight developed between the eastern and western sections, each side declaring itself in favor of dividing the county into two separate counties.[35]

[33] Minutes of Meeting of Summit County Commission, August 1, 1910.

[34] Minutes of Meeting of Millard County Commission, December 7, 1909; February 1, 1910; March 4, 1913.

[35] *Progress-Review*, Fillmore, September 19, 1913, and December 12, 1913.

At its October meeting, the commission voted, two to one, to grant the petitions. Before the formal resolutions of consolidation were passed it was discovered that some of the signers of the petitions were not registered voters, and upon further investigation, the county commission voted in December, 1913 to annul their former action and to postpone consolidation indefinitely.[36] Under the law, approval of registered voters equal in number to a majority of the votes cast in the last general election was required to legalize county school consolidation and the petitioners had failed to secure approval of the required number.

Carbon County. Carbon County became eligible to consolidate its school districts in 1913, and in December of that year the county commission requested the county superintendent to call a meeting of all school officers and the state superintendent of public schools to consider the problem. In the meantime, a controversy arose between the county commission and the school officials over the authority of the commission to audit the books of the county high school district that had been created in 1911.[37] These two issues appear to have become related to each other, and action on consolidation had not been taken by 1915.

Tooele County. Tooele County did not become eligible to consolidate its schools until 1913 and no action toward consolidation was taken prior to the passage of the mandatory law of 1915.

ENACTMENT OF THE MANDATORY LAW

In 1915 pressure from several different sources was concentrated on the state legislature for the purpose of securing the extension of the county school district plan to all counties of the state. At that time, recommendations of the state superintendent of schools were supported by resolutions of the Utah Education Association and by urgent recommendations from the attorney general and the governor.

In each report since 1905, the state superintendent of schools had recommended to each legislature that any county in the

---

[36] Minutes of Meeting of Millard County Commission, December 2, 1913.

[37] Minutes of Meetings of Carbon County Commission, December, 1913; February and May, 1914. See also *Carbon County News*, of Price, Utah, May 14, 1914.

state should have the right to organize a county school district, irrespective of its population. In 1914 Superintendent A. C. Matheson vigorously urged that this change be made and also asked that the legislature remove the requirement that consolidation of schools in a county be petitioned for by a majority of the voters. On the latter point, he said:

In the beginning consolidation was not generally welcomed in any of our eight counties now operating under the plan. In fact, in many cases it was vigorously opposed. It is said that in one county not less than ninety per cent of the citizens opposed it. It is stated, however, on equally reliable authority that today in this same county at least ninety per cent of the people are heartily in favor of consolidation. . . . I cannot too strongly urge an amendment to the law which would soon bring about consolidation in many more counties in the state.[38]

The 1914 report of Attorney General Barnes called the attention of the governor to the existence of three different kinds of school districts in Utah, outside of the cities, which condition was causing legal difficulties that appeared to be increasing. He urged that the county school district of the first class be extended by law to all the counties of the state, thus eliminating the separate high school and elementary school districts. He recommended that one school district only should be required in all counties having less than 5,000 school population.[39]

Influence in favor of extending the county-unit system at this time was also exerted by the Utah Education Association. At its annual convention in Salt Lake City, November 23 to 25, 1914, the association had gone on record as desiring extension of the county-unit plan to all the counties of the state and had instructed its legislative committee to support amendments to that effect in the next session of the legislature.[40]

Possibly influenced by the recommendations of the attorney general, the state superintendent of public instruction, and the Utah Education Association, Governor William Spry made the following recommendation to the legislature on January 18, 1915:

[38] *Tenth Report of the Superintendent of Public Instruction of the State of Utah,* 1914, p. 38.
[39] *Biennial Report of the Attorney General to the Governor of the State of Utah for the Period Ending November 30, 1914,* Salt Lake City, Utah, 1915, pp. 15-19.
[40] *Utah Educational Review,* p. 10, May-June, 1915.

Utah has been gradually working toward the consolidated school district plan and, like the attorney general, the state superintendent of public instruction, and all others who are familiar with the operation of the laws governing the common school system, I am in hearty accord with the consolidation plan. The beneficial results following consolidation in the counties of the state where it has been effected are so manifest that I do not hesitate to recommend an amendment to the law requiring consolidation and removing the barrier against it in counties with a small school population.[41]

After some preliminary discussion between political leaders and educators as to the advisability of passing a mandatory law, such a measure was introduced by the education committee of the house of representatives on February 9, 1915. This bill repealed the local district school law and required organization of a county school district of the first class in each county of the state, except that existing county school districts of the first class were not changed and permission was given to organize existing county high school districts into county school districts of the first class.

The bill, therefore, permitted the creation of more than one school district in five counties of the state. Each of the eight counties that had consolidated under the optional plan, except Salt Lake, had organized only one district in the county. However, after the enactment of the high school law in 1911, two high school districts had been organized in each of Utah, Juab, and Sanpete Counties, and three such districts had been organized in Summit County. In 1915 Juab and Summit Counties each had a relatively small school population, 3,076 and 2,573 respectively. Although each was divided into distinct regions by industrial and physical conditions, it is probable that other counties that were forced to organize on a single district basis were also divided by similar conditions. The real reason why these relatively small counties were allowed to organize two and three school districts under the new law probably was one of expediency. J. Preston Creer, superintendent of schools of Utah County in 1915, and one of the men who worked with the legislature for the enact-

[41] House Journal of Eleventh Session of the Legislature of the State of Utah, 1915, p. 40.

ment of the law, states that certain political leaders of great importance in the legislature, refused to support the measure unless it permitted these counties to divide.[42] Leaders in favor of consolidation desired to secure support for the compulsory feature of the proposed law. Since experience during the past ten years had shown that the people of Summit and Juab Counties wished to have more than one school district in each county, the bill was framed to permit this division.

The bill became a law without serious opposition. The house passed it by a vote of thirty-seven to eight; it was passed by the senate, after minor amendments, without a dissenting vote; and the house concurred in the amendments by a vote of thirty-eight to three.[43]

At the time this law was enacted by the legislature approximately 62 per cent of the people in the state were living in the eight counties in which county-unit school systems had been organized and in the first and second class cities. Only one representative from the eight counties that had adopted the county-unit plan cast a negative vote on the final roll calls in the legislature. Fifty-five per cent of the members of the legislature were from consolidated counties and independent cities. It is probable that the apparent satisfaction of the people with the plan in those counties in which it had been in operation was one of the reasons for the lack of opposition in the legislature to the extension of the county-unit system.

The passage of the mandatory law completed the diffusion of the county-unit school district throughout the state. By the close of 1915, there were five city school districts and thirty-four county school districts in the state. Of the latter, there was one county school district in each of twenty-three counties; two districts in each of four counties; and three districts in one county. The creation of an additional county at a later date necessitated the organization of the latest of the forty public school districts which now exist in the State of Utah.

[42] Personal interview.
[43] *House and Senate Journals of Eleventh Session of the Legislature of the State of Utah*, 1915.

SUMMARY

The school law of 1905 made it permissible for the county commissioners of seven of the twenty-seven counties in the state to organize their local school districts into county school districts of the first class. Growth of population and changes in the law made it permissible for nine other counties to consolidate their schools under this plan prior to 1915.

Eight of these counties created county school districts of the first class. Salt Lake County had consolidated in 1904. The county commissioners of Weber County in 1905, and of Boxelder County in 1907, formed county school districts without serious opposition. In 1908 Cache County commissioners consolidated the district schools, despite strong popular opposition, and in 1908 Morgan County created a county-unit school district as the result of popular vote.

In 1911 the legislature enacted a high school law requiring each county not already organized into county school districts of the first class to organize a county high school district. Following this legislation, Davis and Sevier Counties, which had previously failed in such attempts, organized county school districts for all purposes, rather than create separate high school districts. In 1914 Uintah County secured consent of a majority of its voters to consolidate its school districts.

Prior to 1915 official attempts to organize county school districts in four of the other eligible counties had been unsuccessful. In Sanpete County the final decision was against consolidation, probably because of insufficient taxing power of the county school district. Summit County, in 1910, refused to consolidate because of the division of the county into separate mining and agricultural regions. Millard County, in 1913, failed to secure approval of a majority of the voters, as required under the law at that time. Carbon County was considering consolidation in 1914, but final action had not been taken prior to the passage of the mandatory law in 1915.

Four counties took no official action. Juab and Wasatch were each divided into separate regions by conditions of geography and industry. Tooele had become eligible in 1913 and had not yet considered the problem. In Utah County, which had been eligible to consolidate since 1905, there had never been an official decision of the county commissioners on the problem of consolidation.

Just prior to the meeting of the legislature in 1915, the Utah Education Association, the state superintendent of public instruction, the attorney general, and the governor of the state recommended to the legislature that the county-unit school district be extended to all counties of the state. The legislature enacted a law which made the adoption of the county school district mandatory but also permitted certain counties not yet consolidated to create more than one district in each county.

ANALYTICAL SUMMARY STATEMENTS

In analyzing the process of the development of the county-unit plan in Utah, as related to the diffusion of the county school district throughout the state, the following statements are pertinent to an understanding of the process of adaptation:

1. At no time prior to the enactment of the mandatory law in 1915 had the legislature permitted legal organization of county school districts in counties of comparatively small population.

2. In general, decisions to organize county school districts in Utah prior to 1913 were made by the county commissioners of each county without recourse to popular approval.

3. Consolidation in the five most populous counties that voluntarily accepted it was effected by the county commissioners without knowledge of, or in opposition to, the will of the people in the county.

4. The only counties that accepted the county-unit school district as a result of approval of a majority of voters were two of the three least populous counties that were eligible to consolidate and in each of these counties there was only one incorporated town, which was the county seat.

5. Except in Salt Lake County, each county that accepted the county-unit plan during the optional period organized only one school district. The five counties that were eligible to consolidate

by 1911, but did not consolidate, all formed more than one high school district within the county at that time and in 1915 organized a county school district for each high school unit. These facts suggest that certain undetermined factors, associated with county unity, were related to the early acceptance of the county school district of the first class.

6. The outstanding reason given for consolidation of school districts in the records of county commissions was the desire to equalize educational opportunity by the equalizing of school revenue.

7. Passage of the high school law in 1911 seemed to hasten the creation of county school districts of the first class in counties that had previously given the problem serious consideration. Sanpete County, the one exception, probably would have consolidated at this time if the tax limitation law had not seriously restricted the taxing power of the consolidated district.

8. The legislature enacted a state-wide mandatory law in 1911 for the organization of special high school districts. Prior to 1915 the legislature had restricted the acceptance of the county-unit school district to the counties of comparatively large population. This fact indicates that the legislature considered the organization of the high school district to be a more urgent problem than the consolidation of districts for all purposes.

9. It is probable that inclusion of a member from each local district on the board of education of the high school districts tended to decrease opposition to consolidation for all school purposes.

10. There is an apparent contradiction between the action of the legislature in 1913 in requiring approval of a majority of the voters in a county before permitting the county commissioners to organize a county school district, and the action of the legislature in 1915 in forcing the county-unit system on all counties by mandatory law. It is possible that the general popular approval of the county-unit plan in those counties in which it had been in operation convinced the legislature that consolidation would eventually receive similar support in other counties of the state.

CHAPTER V

FACTORS INFLUENCING THE DEVELOPMENT OF THE COUNTY-UNIT SCHOOL DISTRICT IN UTAH

THE causes of social change are so complex and the possibility of studying single factors which cause change, independent of the influence of other factors, is so remote that it is seldom possible to state with accuracy the extent to which any single factor influences a particular adaptation. However, it is desirable to identify the factors which are associated with a particular process of change and to analyze probable relationships existing between these factors and the change which has occurred. The completion of many studies of individual adaptations may then reveal common factors associated with these adaptations and permit a valid formulation of principles and procedures that control certain types of change in education.

For purposes of ease of classification with other studies in adaptability and for convenience of treatment, factors which may have influenced the adoption of the county-unit school district in the state of Utah will be considered in three general groups, as presented by Mort and Cornell,[1] as follows: (1) factors not directly subject to administrative control, (2) factors in the school organization affecting the process of change, and (3) agencies and devices used in the adaptation process.

Certain of these factors, such as density of population, incorporated areas in counties, and need of high school facilities, have been suggested by the study of individual counties in previous chapters. Analysis of other factors, such as age distribution of population and racial composition of population, have been suggested by other studies in adaptability and data on these factors have been presented so that the present study may contribute more fully to these studies in the general field of adaptability.

[1] Mort and Cornell, *Adaptability of Public School Systems,* Chap. IV.

FACTORS NOT SUBJECT TO ADMINISTRATIVE CONTROL

Some elements in the environment associated with the adoption of the county-unit school district in Utah are fairly static, for example, the physical features of the territory and the size of counties. Other elements in the environment, for example, characteristics of the population, are constantly undergoing change and thus tend to require change in educational institutions in order to prevent maladjustment. In considering certain of these factors of the environment which are not directly subject to administrative control of education, but which are associated with the adoption of the county-unit school district in Utah, analysis is made of differences in these factors which exist between the group of eight counties that adopted the county-unit school district prior to 1915 and the group of eight counties that did not adopt the system. Data relating to these differences between the two groups of counties are shown in three tables, reference to which will be made in the following sections. For convenience, the counties which consolidated their schools will be designated as Group A and the eight counties which did not consolidate their schools will be designated as Group B.

Size of Counties. In 1910 there were twenty-seven counties in Utah, with an average area of 3,044 square miles. The average size of the Group A counties was 2,002 square miles, 57 per cent as large as the average county that did not consolidate. Of the sixteen eligible counties, the five having the smallest area adopted consolidation. However, Boxelder and Uintah, both of which adopted consolidation, are among the largest counties of the state. Three of the counties that did not consolidate are smaller in area than three of the counties that did consolidate. Therefore, although the counties which consolidated tended to be those of the smallest areas this was not a characteristic common to all counties of that group.

Counties as Geographic Units. In general, the division lines between counties in Utah are natural boundaries, such as mountains, streams, and lakes. Almost without exception, in the populated sections of the state the county boundaries are natural

TABLE II

DATA RELATING TO CERTAIN CHARACTERISTICS OF AREA, WEALTH, AND POPULATION OF TWO GROUPS OF UTAH COUNTIES IN 1910[a]

Item	Eight Counties Adopting County Unit	Eight Counties Not Adopting County Unit	State
1. Average area of counties in square miles	2,002	3,520	3,044
2. Total population	233,044	105,134	373,351
3. Population, exclusive of independent cities	107,165	96,209	238,547
4. Density of population per square mile ..	14.5	3.7	4.5
5. Density of population per square mile of farm land	108	51	71
6. Density of population per square mile of farm land, exclusive of independent cities	50	46	45
7. Assessed valuation of property per school census child (6 to 18 years of age), exclusive of independent cities	1,681	1,516	1,716
8. School expenditures, per school census child (6 to 18 years of age), for operating expenses exclusive of independent cities[b]	15.05	15.25	15.26
9. Per cent of foreign born whites, exclusive of independent cities	17.8	16.2	17.0
10. Per cent of children (6 to 20 years of age), exclusive of independent cities	33.8	33.3	32.4
11. Per cent increase in population, 1900 to 1910	49.3	15.4	34.9
12. Per cent increase in population, 1900 to 1910, exclusive of independent cities	32.7	13.3	22.2
13. Per cent increase in public elementary school enrollment, 1900 to 1910, exclusive of independent cities	16.6[c]	12.0	11.3
14. Per cent increase in public high school enrollment, 1900 to 1910, exclusive of independent cities	894.7	919.8	926.8

[a] Data for completion of items 7, 8, 13, and 14, taken from *Utah State School Reports*, 1900–1901 and 1910–1911. Data for other items taken from *Thirteenth Census of the United States*, 1910.

[b] Expenditures for the five counties that consolidated prior to 1910 were taken from 1905 reports and weighted by ratio of 1.46, which represented per capita increase of school expenditures in the state between 1905 and 1910.

[c] This figure would probably approach 25 per cent if data for number of children lost to Salt Lake County by extension of incorporated area of Salt Lake City had been available.

division lines, such as mountain valleys and their subsidiary territory. The straight lines which appear on the map as division lines of counties occur in the sparsely settled wastelands of the state.

There appears to be no material difference between the two groups of counties being considered with regard to the division of the counties into natural geographical units.

Density of Population. If all population is included, there is a material difference in the density of population between the two groups. The Group A counties contain four times as many people per square mile as those of Group B. However, when the waste areas of the counties are eliminated from consideration by computing the density of population according to square miles of farm land, the Group A counties have only twice as dense a population as those in Group B. Since all of the first and second class cities are found in the sixteen counties under consideration and since these cities are independent school districts, separate from the county school districts, the fairest basis of comparison is probably that of the population actually residing in the area of the county school district. Item six of Table II shows that the population of the two groups of counties, when measured according to the number of people per square mile of farm land, exclusive of the population of independent cities, is approximately equal.

Among individual counties, the same general conclusion is reached. Salt Lake County, which had the largest rural population of the sixteen counties under consideration, is in Group A, but the next two largest counties in population, Utah and Sanpete, are in Group B. The difference in density of population of the territory included in the county school district, exclusive of cities, does not appear to have been a significant factor that influenced the process of consolidation.

Age Distribution. The percentage of children of ages six to twenty years, exclusive of cities of the first and second class, is approximately equal for the two groups of counties, indicating that the factor of age distribution of the population is not a significant factor.

Racial Distribution. The number of people other than those of the white race in Utah is comparatively insignificant. A comparison of the per cent of foreign born in the two groups of counties shows 17.8 per cent of the population in the Group A counties and 16.2 per cent of the population in the Group B counties to be foreign born. It is doubtful if this small difference would be significant in influencing the adoption of the county-unit school district.

Rate of Population Growth. It is probable that the rate of population growth was a factor which influenced the adoption of the consolidated school district. During the period from 1900 to 1910 the counties in Group A increased in rural population 32.7 per cent, while the counties in Group B increased 13.3 per cent. During this period the population of Salt Lake County, not including Salt Lake City, increased 60 per cent.

These increases in population were accompanied by increased elementary and high school enrollment, as shown by data presented in items 13 and 14 of Table II. The rapid increase of population in counties of Group A, as compared with those of Group B, appears to have been an important factor which influenced the adoption of the county-unit school district in Utah.

Maximum Period of Population Increase. It may be significant that there was a greater increase of population in Utah during the decade 1900 to 1910 than during the decades immediately preceding and immediately following that period. The per cent of increase from 1890 to 1900 was 31.3; from 1900 to 1910, 34.9; and from 1910 to 1920, 20.4. Sufficient data are not available in this study to estimate the effect, if any, that this fact might have had on the development of the county-unit school district.

Proximity to Large Cities. The fact that the first five counties to consolidate their school districts either contained, or were near, independent city school districts illustrates an important factor which probably influenced consolidation. Throughout the history of the county-unit school district in Utah, from the time of John R. Park's first state report of 1896 to the recommendation of Governor Spry to the legislature in 1915, the school districts of the first and second class cities in Utah were pointed to as examples of the efficiency of large units for school administration. The first county consolidation took place in Salt Lake County, which contained Salt Lake City, the largest city in the state; the second district was organized in Weber County, which contained Ogden, the second largest city in the state; the third consolidation was in Boxelder County, which borders on Weber County and the principal city of which is only twenty miles from Ogden. Cache County, the fourth consolidated district, contains Logan, the fourth largest city in the state; and Morgan County borders on Weber County to the west and is near Salt Lake County. The fact that Utah County, which contains Provo, the third largest city in the state, did not consolidate was probably due to the presence of several large towns in the county which were able to offer advantages of good graded schools and high school education to a large portion of the children of that county. Data are presented in Chapter III showing that the desire to offer high school education to the children of Salt Lake County, without requiring them to go to Salt Lake City to secure it, was one of the factors which brought about the first county consolidation. There can be little doubt that the proximity of large cities which contained efficient school systems was an important factor in bringing about consolidation in the counties near those cities.

Proximity to Centers of Higher Education. During the process of the adoption of the county school district, Utah had two public institutions of higher education, the University of Utah at Salt Lake City and the Utah State Agricultural College at Logan. There is evidence that professors from both institutions took part in the process of consolidation. When John R. Park first suggested the idea of a county unit, he was President of the University of Utah (then called Deseret) and he presented the idea of the county unit to his students at the University.[2] As early as 1888, Park explained his theory to an institute of teachers in Salt Lake County.[3] Matheson and Moss report that professors from the University of Utah assisted in the campaign for the con-

---

[2] Written testimony in Minutes of Morgan County Commission, June 30, 1907.

[3] *Thirty-Fifth Annual Report of the State Superintendent of Public Instruction of the State of New York,* 1889. Appendix, p. 189.

version of the school trustees in Salt Lake County to the idea of the county-unit school system.[4] During the summer of 1911, Professor E. P. Cubberley, in the summer school at the University of Utah, vigorously criticized Utah for not making more rapid progress with the county-unit plan.[5] Professor George Thomas of the Utah State Agricultural College appeared before the Cache County commission and urged the commissioners to consolidate the schools of that county.[6]

It is evident that representatives of the higher institutions of learning participated in the movement for consolidation of schools. It is probable that this was a factor which influenced the process of consolidation.

Wealth. Data in item 7 of Table II show that the average assessed valuation of property per school child was approximately 10 per cent greater in counties of Group A than in those of Group B. The extent to which this difference in wealth actually operated as a factor that influenced the process of consolidation is not evident.

Private and Parochial Schools. Although there were a number of private and denominational schools in Utah during the period from 1905 to 1915, the only such schools that enrolled an appreciable number of children were those that were maintained by the "Mormon" Church. During the school year 1905–1906 ten schools were maintained by this church in Utah, all of which offered high school courses, three of which offered college work, and none of which were open to children of elementary age.[7]

These church schools were established between 1875 and 1879, and prior to 1900 they, together with two small academies maintained by other protestant sects, were the only secondary schools available to children of the state outside the cities of Salt Lake, Ogden, and Logan. By taking care of the early needs for high school education in the rural sections of the state, these church schools may have delayed the demand for public high schools. On the other hand, the existence of these schools in certain

[4] Interviews with A. C. Matheson and James E. Moss.
[5] *Utah Educational Review*, September, 1911, p. 7.
[6] Minutes of Meeting of Cache County Commission, March 23, 1908.
[7] Biennial State School Report, 1906, *op. cit.*, pp. 446-451.

communities may have been a factor in creating dissatisfaction with the lack of high school facilities in other sections of the state, and thus have indirectly contributed to the demand for school district consolidation.

Incorporated Areas in Counties. The extent to which the population of the two groups of counties was included in incorporated villages, towns, and third class cities was probably an important factor which influenced the movement for school district consolidation. In the counties of Group A only 26 per cent of the people were included in these incorporated towns as compared

TABLE III

PER CENT OF POPULATION IN INCORPORATED VILLAGES, TOWNS, AND CITIES IN SIXTEEN UTAH COUNTIES

(Exclusive of First and Second Class Cities, for United States Census Year Next Preceding Date Each County Became Eligible to Adopt County-Unit School Districts[a])

Counties That Consolidated (Group A)	Number of Towns with Population above 1,000	Per Cent of Population in Incorporated Units	Counties Not Consolidated (Group B)	Number of Towns with Population above 1,000	Per Cent of Population in Incorporated Units
Salt Lake ..	1	4.2	Utah	6	72.8
Weber	0	0.0	Sanpete	6	73.1
Boxelder ...	1	41.2	Juab	3	80.9
Cache	3	54.8	Wasatch ...	1	35.3
Morgan	0	29.3	Summit	1	53.8
Davis	2	51.6	Carbon	1	34.1
Sevier	3	63.6	Millard	1	51.2
Uintah	0	11.8	Tooele	3	68.9
Total	10	25.9	Total	22	63.2

[a] Data for counties of Salt Lake, Weber, Boxelder, Cache, Morgan, Davis, Sevier, Utah, and Sanpete are taken from *Twelfth Census of the United States*, 1900, Vol. I. Data for other counties are taken from *Thirteenth Census of the United States*, 1910, Vol. III.

with 63 per cent of the population in Group B. Each of these incorporated areas, with two exceptions, contained only one school district and was large enough to maintain graded elementary schools. Data in Table III show that only ten towns in Group A exceeded one thousand population, the legal size necessary to establish a high school, while twenty-two towns in Group B exceeded this population limit.

Consideration of individual counties also indicates that this factor affected consolidation. In Group A the three counties having the largest per cent of people in incorporated areas—Cache, Davis, and Sevier—were counties in which the people had indicated opposition to consolidation. Cache County was consolidated against the wishes of the people and Davis County and Sevier County had refused to consolidate prior to the passing of the high school district law in 1911. Of the Group B counties, each of the two that had been eligible to consolidate in 1905, when the county district law was passed, had high percentages of incorporated areas. The evidence indicates that a high percentage of population living in incorporated towns within a county was an unfavorable factor for consolidation.

Religious Composition of Counties. Because a majority of people in Utah are members of one church, inquiry was made as to possible relationships between this condition and the development of the county-unit school district. No evidence was found that the church organization had given direct support, either for or against consolidation. Persons who were interviewed were unanimous in their belief that consolidation had not been made a religious issue.

Data presented in Table IV tend to show that per cent of membership in the dominant church was not a factor that favored the adoption of the county school district. There was a lower per cent of "Mormon" population in the counties of Group A than in the counties of Group B. In Group A the three counties having the highest per cent of "Mormon" population were the three in which the people showed the greatest opposition to consolidation. In Group B, Utah and Sanpete Counties, the only two that were eligible to consolidate throughout the entire period from 1905 to 1915, had the highest per cent of "Mormon" population of the counties that did not consolidate.

Additional evidence on this factor is that during the period that school districts were being consolidated in Utah the policy of the church was to subdivide the local units in the church organi-

TABLE IV

PER CENT OF POPULATION IN SIXTEEN UTAH COUNTIES ELIGIBLE
TO ADOPT COUNTY-UNIT SCHOOL DISTRICT THAT WERE MEMBERS
OF DOMINANT CHURCH, 1910[a]

Counties That Consolidated (Group A)	Per Cent in Dominant Church	Counties Not Consolidated (Group B)	Per Cent in Dominant Church
Salt Lake	41.0	Utah	75.1
Weber	50.0	Sanpete	87.0
Boxelder	73.1	Juab	48.9
Cache	90.5	Wasatch	55.8
Morgan	72.1	Summit	52.7
Davis	74.6	Carbon	29.2
Sevier	82.8	Millard	74.1
Uintah	56.3	Tooele	45.9
Total	53.2	Total	64.9

[a] Compiled from population data contained in *Thirteenth Census of United States,* 1910, Vol. III, and church membership data in records which are available in the church historian's office, Church of Jesus Christ of Latter Day Saints, Salt Lake City, Utah.

zation. From 1905 to 1915 the number of stakes in these sixteen counties increased from twenty-three to thirty and the number of wards increased from 259 to 327.

There is evidence, however, that the organization of the dominant church had some indirect effect upon the county-unit organization of schools. Evidence is presented in Chapter III to show that the existing organization of the church in Salt Lake County may have influenced the decision to create two consolidated school districts in that county instead of one. Salt Lake, in 1905, and Utah and Sanpete Counties, in 1915, each organized two county school districts which coincided geographically with, and took the same names as, the stakes of the "Mormon" Church already existing in those areas. On the other hand, Boxelder and Cache Counties each created only one school district, although there were two or more church stakes in each county. In 1915, although there was only one church stake in Juab and Summit Counties, each organized more than one county school district.

The evidence indicates that there was no direct influence of the dominant church that favored consolidation of school districts, and is conflicting as to the extent to which the dominant church organization may have indirectly influenced it.

Local Authority to Create School Districts. The relationship existing between state and local authority in the organization of school districts in Utah was an important factor affecting the development of the county-unit plan. The creation and consolidation of school districts had been delegated by the legislature of the territory of Utah to the county court, which was the elected governmental body of control for the lowest civil unit of government common to all the territory. Until 1890 all school districts that were organized were governed by boards of local trustees, to whom the law gave control practically independent of state and county school officials. When it was thought desirable to create a separate type of school district for cities of the first and second class, this was done by legislative act in 1890. Separate school districts for these cities was made a constitutional provision when Utah became a state in 1896.

It is probable that prior to 1905 those who advocated the adoption of the county-unit school district had assumed that this would be an entirely different type of district from those in existence at that time, and that the county-unit district could not be created except by a special act of the legislature. This would account for the assumption in all references to the county unit that the first step necessary to secure its adoption was the enactment of a special law. The creation of a school district of this kind was first achieved by action of the Salt Lake County officials on the assumption that they had the authority to create a large school district by consolidation and could operate it, if necessary, under the existing law. The purpose of the act which they secured from the 1905 legislature was not to grant additional powers for the creation of county school districts, but to increase the authority of such districts after they had been created.

It is important, in this regard, to note that the legislature of 1905 did not limit the power of the county commission to consolidate school districts. This unlimited power of a local representative body was an important factor in the consolidation process.

ELEMENTS OF SCHOOL ORGANIZATION INFLUENCING
THE PROCESS OF ADAPTATION

Certain factors which affected the process of consolidation were elements of the school organization and somewhat subject to school control.

Need of High School Facilities. The desire of educators and of the public to secure opportunities for high school education for all children in the state probably was a major factor in securing the adoption of the county-unit school district. The desire to secure high schools in Salt Lake County in 1904 and the passage in 1911 of a special county high school law were closely related to the development of the county-unit plan, as is explained in Chapters III and IV of this study. It is probable that county school consolidation would not have been effected in Utah if a practical solution to the high school problem had been effected prior to 1904.

Distinction between Attendance and Administrative Units. Throughout the period of diffusion of the county-unit district in Utah there appears to have been practically no attempt to make the attendance unit coincide with the administrative unit. As is shown in Chapter III, the distinction between these two was made by Salt Lake County in 1904 and it appears to have set a precedent by which the limitations of school transportation did not enter materially as a factor in determining the size of the school district.

School Expenditures. It has been shown that the counties of Group A had a higher assessed valuation per capita than the counties of Group B. Data presented in item 8 of Table II show that the per capita expenditures of the two groups were approximately equal. This would indicate that, in general, the counties that consolidated were making less financial effort to maintain their schools than were the counties that did not consolidate. Data on which to base an interpretation of this situation were not available to the investigator.

Method of Finance. The method of finance for the support of schools in Utah during the period of the diffusion of the county-unit school district was a combination of local and general support. The state government levied a three mill tax on the property valuation of the state, and the proceeds of the tax, together with revenue from the permanent school fund, were distributed to the districts on a per capita basis. For the school year 1904–1905, this amounted to 22 per cent of the total receipts of the school districts outside the independent cities.[8] The remainder of the school revenue was raised within the county, either by a county or by a local tax. For the school year 1904–1905, the counties of Group A raised $2.91 per school child from the county-wide tax and the counties of Group B raised $2.47 from this source. Since the revenue from the state, $4.61 per school child, was equal for all the counties, these data show that the counties that did not consolidate were raising a higher proportion of their school revenue from local school district sources in the school year 1904–1905 than were the counties that consolidated their schools. For both groups of counties, approximately 65 per cent of the revenue was being raised from sources within the local school district.

It is highly probable that the proportion of total school revenue which was raised from local district sources was an important factor in creating a demand for school district consolidation in many Utah counties.

Degree of Local Tax Freedom. The school laws from 1905 to 1915 permitted the trustees of a local school district to levy a local tax of ten mills for elementary school purposes and a high school tax of five mills if the population was large enough to be a high school district. By special vote of the taxpayers the elementary school rate could be raised to twenty mills. In addition to the local taxes a county school tax rate of four mills could be levied. These laws applied equally to all counties in the state.[9]

The county school law of 1905 limited the tax rate for county districts to seven mills for elementary school purposes and five mills for high schools. For two years, from 1911 to 1913, the right to levy the high school tax was taken away from the county district. The county district therefore had less tax freedom than the

---

[8] Biennial State School Report, 1906, *op. cit.*, Statistical Tables, p. 33.
[9] *Compiled Laws of Utah*, 1907, p. 697.

local school district, and this limitation of taxing power probably was a factor in retarding the diffusion of the county-unit school district.

State and Local Leadership. There can be little doubt that the influence of personal leadership was an important factor in securing the adoption of the county-unit school district in Utah. The devotion of John R. Park to the idea of a county-unit district and the persistence with which he kept the idea before the educators of the state doubtless was a major factor in the conversion of educational leaders and many lay leaders to the county-unit plan. The fact that the power to consolidate schools was held by a group of three men in each county emphasizes the importance of the factor of personal leadership in the process of the adaptation. Relating to social situations of this kind, Allport says:

In many face-to-face groups, such as committees and other constructive bodies, social behavior takes the form of securing adjustments of ascendance and submission among the members. Each asserts his opinion as to what should be done, and supports it by suggestion, by logic, or by the domination of his personality. Final decision in the adoption of a plan may come by discussion, persuasion, compromise, or sheer majority. In any case, however, the struggle for personal ascendancy looms large. The conclusion arrived at is as likely to be the result of control by ascendant personalities as of rational planning.[10]

The work of B. W. Ashton and his colleagues in securing the first large school district consolidation in Salt Lake County consisted of meetings with small "face-to-face" groups. Ability to win the support of individual commissioners in a county sometimes appeared to be the deciding factor in the decision to consolidate. Although it is difficult to appraise the extent to which personal leadership contributed to the process of consolidation, it seems certain that the character and energy of this leadership was a major factor in the process.

AGENCIES AND DEVICES USED IN THE PROCESS OF ADAPTATION

The more important agencies and devices which were used in Utah to influence the process of adaptation are listed below in

[10] F. H. Allport, *Social Psychology,* p. 286. Boston: Houghton Mifflin Co., 1924.

summary form with brief notes of explanation. More detailed explanations of how these agencies and devices were used are in the preceding chapters of this study. In only a few instances is additional evidence presented in this section.

I. Official and quasi-official agencies
  A. National agencies
    1. United States Bureau of Education
      a. In 1913 a representative of the bureau made a study of the consolidation of County districts of Utah.[11] This study received considerable attention in the state among educators and probably was a factor in securing the passage of the mandatory law in 1915.
    2. National Education Association
      a. Meetings of this organization held in 1913 and in 1914 endorsed the county-unit school district. The 1913 meeting was held in Salt Lake City and probably influenced the Utah Education Association to take a positive stand for consolidation in 1914.[12]
  B. State agencies
    1. State universities
      a. Although the state universities did not act in an official capacity as agents for county school consolidation, various members of their staffs worked publicly for consolidation.
    2. State government agencies
      a. Reports of the State Department of Public Instruction, 1881 to 1915.
      b. Visits of state school officers at institutes and local meetings.
      c. Report of state attorney general, 1914.
      d. Governor's message to legislature, 1915.
  C. Local agencies
    1. Reports of county superintendents to the State Department of Education

---

[11] *Utah Educational Review,* December, 1913, p. 26.
[12] *Ibid.,* September-November, 1913, p. 23.

2. Visits of county superintendent with trustees and teachers

3. Official committees

   a. Nearly all county commissions that considered consolidation after 1905 appointed committees to study the results in other counties where it was being tried.

II. Non-official agencies

  A. National agencies

    1. Prominent national individuals

      a. The speeches of Cubberley at the summer sessions of the University of Utah in 1911 probably influenced the process.[13]

  B. State agencies

    1. State Teachers Association

      a. Mathonihah Thomas, as president of the Association, in 1910 advocated county consolidation in his annual address to the Association.[14]

      b. Official resolutions passed in 1914.

      c. Articles and news notes in *Utah Educational Review.*

  C. Local agencies

    1. Local institutes of teachers

      a. John R. Park explained idea to Salt Lake County teachers in 1888.

      b. Resolutions of Cache County teachers in 1908.

    2. Citizens' committees

    3. Protest meetings

    4. Petitions to county commissions

    5. Mass meetings of citizens

    6. Prominent individuals

      a. Appearance before meetings of citizens and of county commissioners.

III. Other devices used in process of adaptation

  A. State and local newspaper publicity

    1. News articles

[13] *Ibid.*, September, 1911, p. 7.
[14] *Ibid.*, February, 1911, p. 10.

  2. Editorials

B. Introduction of laws in the legislature

  1. In 1888, although the law was defeated, the amount of publicity secured in the papers probably helped to diffuse the idea.

  2. In 1905 acquaintance with the law in the legislature probably influenced legislators to encourage its adoption in Weber and Boxelder Counties.

  3. Amendments to the law in 1911 and 1913 probably helped to secure favorable action toward the mandatory law of 1915.

SUMMARY

The counties of the state which voluntarily consolidated during the period from 1905 to 1915 (Group A) were smaller in average area, were nearer the larger cities, and were in closer proximity to the state institutions of higher education than were the counties that did not consolidate (Group B). The counties in Group A had a much lower per cent of their population residing in incorporated villages, towns, and cities than did the counties of Group B.

Counties in Group A had a per cent of increase in population during the decade preceding their consolidation nearly three times as great as the per cent of increase which the Group B counties had between 1900 and 1910. The two groups of counties did not show a material difference in density of population as measured by rural population per square mile of farm land. The counties of Group A had approximately a 10 per cent greater assessed valuation per school child than the counties of Group B.

It is probable that the existence of private and religious schools in the state did not materially influence the development of the county-unit school district, except that the existence of academies of the dominant church may have taken care of early needs for high school education. The evidence that is available tends to show that the factor of membership of a majority of the population in one church was not a major influence in the development of the county-unit school district. One major influential factor probably was the possession of authority by the county commission of each county to consolidate school districts without recourse to popular approval.

There was little difference between the two groups of counties in per capita school expenditures, although the fact that 65 per cent of school revenue was raised from local sources probably contributed to a desire to consolidate school districts in order to equalize the burden of taxation. It is probable that the diffusion of the county-unit plan was retarded by the more restricted taxing power that the county school district possessed, as compared with the taxing power of the local school districts.

Two factors of major importance in influencing the development of the county school district were the need of high school facilities in the rural areas of the state and the effectiveness of personal leadership in securing favorable action toward consolidation by the county commissioners of the various counties and by the legislature.

A list of agencies and devices used in the process of adaptation shows a wide variety of national, state, and local agencies, official and non-official in character. In some instances these devices were used for exercising control, but in most instances persons or institutions consciously directed the process of adaptation.

CHAPTER VI

THE PATTERN OF ADAPTATION

THE development of the county-unit school district in the state of Utah was the result of the interaction of many social forces with each other and with the social institutions through which these forces sought to find expression. The process of development was not one of uninterrupted progress. The earliest school district consolidations occurred in cities as a result of local initiative and were later made uniform for first and second class cities by state law. A large-unit consolidation of rural school districts was first suggested by state school officials and an unsuccessful attempt was made to secure the enactment of a mandatory law requiring the organization of county-unit school districts in all counties. A revised plan for a large rural school district was later adopted by a county in an attempt to solve pressing school problems. The plan was legalized by the legislature and was adopted by other counties, after which the legislature, as a result of the experience of these counties, made the county-unit school district mandatory for all counties of the state.

ADAPTATION PATTERN FOR THE COUNTY-UNIT SCHOOL DISTRICT

Certain general steps, or periods of development, in the process of adaptation can be identified and are here organized into a pattern of adaptation:

1. Division of counties into local school districts, 1854–1915.
2. Expression of need of larger school units, 1871–1880.
3. Consolidation of districts in cities, 1872–1890.
4. Emergence of idea of county-unit district, 1881.
5. Attempt to establish county-unit districts by mandatory law, 1888.
6. Creation of new organization for school districts of first and second class cities, 1890.

7. Revision of county-unit proposals, based on city school experience, 1896.
8. Growth of local demand for county school districts, 1896–1905.
9. First organization of large county school districts, 1905.
10. Legal authorization of special school organization for large rural districts, 1905.
11. Limited diffusion of county-unit district by local initiative, 1905–1914.
12. Complete diffusion of county-unit district by mandatory law, 1915.

TIME INTERVALS BETWEEN STAGES

The time elapsing between the first noted expression of the need of larger school units and the emergence of the county-unit idea in Utah was ten years, the period from 1871 to 1881. The time lapse between the emergence of the county-unit idea and the first county school district organization was twenty-four years, from 1881 to 1905. The period of diffusion in Utah was ten years, from 1905 to 1915.

OTHER PATTERNS OF EDUCATIONAL ADAPTATIONS

Other patterns of adaptations in public school systems have been suggested by Cubberley, Mort, and Farnsworth.

Cubberley found the following general pattern to be operative in the process of securing state supported free public schools.[1]

1. Permission granted to communities so desiring to organize a school taxing district, and to tax for school support the property of those consenting and residing therein.
2. Taxation of all property in the taxing unit permitted.
3. State aid to such districts; at first from the income of permanent endowment funds, and later from the proceeds of a small state appropriation or a state or county tax.
4. Compulsory local taxation to supplement the state or county grant.

[1] E. P. Cubberley, *The History of Education,* p. 678. Boston: Houghton Mifflin Co., 1920.

This pattern is concerned, in general, with provision for financial support and control, since the adaptation was one which was possible only by the raising of large amounts of revenue for the support of schools.

On the basis of Cubberley's studies, and several independent studies in parts of South Africa and the United States, Mort and Cornell have suggested a typical local initiative pattern for public school adaptations in the United States:[2]

1. Origin in a local community, often without knowledge of state officials.
2. Diffusion to other communities, usually with encouragement of state school officials.
3. Permissive legislation secured, if necessary or desirable.
4. Special state aid is often secured.
5. Mandatory legislation is secured to speed up diffusion.

The order of steps 1, 2, and 3 in the process is not often the same, for special aid sometimes appears near the beginning of the process, often as an accompaniment of permissive legislation. At times the permissive legislation precedes the diffusion of the adaptation. The suggested pattern was intended to be general and hypothetical, subject to verification or modification by results of subsequent studies.

Another pattern of adaptation has been stated by Farnsworth for the development of five public school services in three northeastern states, as follows:[3]

1. Some condition accentuated the need.
2. A leader recognized and made the need articulate.
3. Solutions were proposed to ameliorate conditions.
4. Trial attempts at solution were undertaken.
5. Financial aid from private, local, or state sources helped in the introduction of the service.
6. Studies of conditions were made.
7. Official approval was sought.

[2] Mort and Cornell, *Adaptability of Public School Systems*, p. 71.
[3] Philo T. Farnsworth, "Adaptation Processes in Public School Systems." Dissertation awaiting publication, Teachers College, Columbia University, New York. p. 171.

8. Lay and professional groups, as well as prominent individuals, advocated official approval.

9. An agency was designated to promote and supervise activities.

10. Some form of state stimulation followed.

The adaptations which Farnsworth studied were of school services for atypical children, vocational education, library service, rural supervision, and medical inspection, all of which involved additional expenditure of funds and some of which were carried on by other agencies before they became school functions.

SIGNIFICANT DIFFERENCES BETWEEN THE PATTERNS

Probably because of the nature of the individual adaptations being studied, the adaptation pattern for Utah county school districts is different from the other patterns of adaptation in two significant respects. One is that the origin and early development of the idea of the county school district was associated with state school officials and did not assume the local initiative pattern until fifteen years after it was first suggested. This may have been due to the nature of the adaptation. Officers who were visiting all the school districts of a state would be more likely to notice differences in the efficiency of large and small districts and to seek a solution for the weaknesses observed. Since the school district was a creation of the state it probably was natural for the state school officials to seek consolidation of districts by state law even though consolidation of districts in several cities had already taken place on a voluntary basis.

The second difference is that at no time was the device of special state financial aid used in Utah to encourage the diffusion of the county school district. On the contrary, the laws which regulated these special county districts actually gave them less taxing power than was possessed by the local school districts which they replaced. The nature of the adaptation did not require additional expenditure for its adoption. In fact, it was expected to operate either with less total cost or to secure greater efficiency with an equal expenditure of funds. The reason for the omission of special aid from the general pattern of this adaptation is probably that this adaptation was different in type from other adaptations that have been studied. This innovation is not an addition to school services rendered by the school organization, but is a change in the school organization itself.

SIMILARITY TO PATTERN OF LOCAL INITIATIVE

Other than the differences in the origin of the idea and the device of stimulation of diffusion by special aid, there is great similarity between the county school district pattern and those discussed in previous studies. The last four steps of the former, after it assumed a local initiative stage of development, fully agree with the general local initiative pattern of Mort and Cornell, except for the item of special aid. There is no essential difference between the county school district pattern and those of Cubberley and Farnsworth, except in the two steps which have been explained.

The present study therefore supports the general local initiative pattern of previous studies and suggests that variations may be expected in the pattern of development of individual adaptations as a result of the variations in the nature of these adaptations and of the environment in which they develop.

CHAPTER VII

SUMMARY AND CONCLUSIONS

IN THE preceding chapters the findings of the investigation have shown the process of development of the county-unit school district in Utah; the pattern, or mode of change, which the process followed; and the factors which appear to have influenced the process of development, including agencies and devices which were used in the process.

It has been shown that the authority to consolidate school districts in Utah was delegated to the executive officers of each county shortly after the territory was organized; that the need of consolidation of districts was first recognized in the cities and the earliest consolidations took place there; and that the first suggestion that county school districts should be created was made by agents of the territorial school office, probably by John R. Park. Park and other central school officials for many years advocated the establishing of county school districts on the assumption that the first necessary step was the enactment of a mandatory or a permissive law by the legislature. By 1905 the legislature had failed to take action on the problem.

From 1900 to 1904 there was a growing consciousness in the state of the need of high schools in areas outside of cities of the first and second class. Attempts to form union high school districts under the existing law had failed. In 1904, pursuant to a request of B. W. Ashton, county superintendent of schools, the county commission of Salt Lake County consolidated the rural school districts of that county into two school districts. A special committee was successful in securing legislation which gave county school districts with 3,000 or more children the same general organization and authority as that held by school districts in second class cities. Amendments to the law made it permissible for sixteen counties to organize county school districts of the first class prior to 1915, at which time the county school district was made mandatory for all counties of the state. Prior to this date the county commissions of eight counties had voluntarily consolidated their school districts, generally without popular approval.

Analysis of factors which appeared to be characteristic of the group of counties that consolidated, as compared with the factors considered characteristic of the group of counties that did not consolidate, shows that the counties that consolidated were smaller in area; that they had a more rapid growth of population during the census period preceding their eligibility to consolidate; that a relatively small per cent of their people lived in incorporated towns or cities; that they were in close proximity to the state universities; and that they were near the larger cities of the state. There were minor differences between the counties in the density of rural population per square mile of farm land, the per cent of total population that were of school age, the assessed valuation of property per school child, per capita school expenditures, and the proportion of school revenue raised from local sources, but these differences do not appear to have been significant.

Several factors existing in the general state situation appear to have favored the development of the county-unit school district in the state. The division lines between counties in the populated areas generally followed natural division lines. Between 1895 and 1910 there was a growing need for organization of high schools and the authority to create high school districts had proved to be ineffective. The possession by county officers of authority to consolidate school districts was an important element in the situation. Throughout the period of development of the county-unit district the effectiveness of state and local leadership in furthering the progress of adaptation appears to have been a vital factor.

The division of some counties into two or more separate regions because of conditions of geography and industry, and the more restricted taxing power of the county-unit district appear to have been factors that retarded its development. The membership of a majority of the people of Utah in one church does not appear to have been a significant factor in the development of the county-unit district.

The underlying factor that appears to have favored the passage of the mandatory law was the apparent popular approval of the county-unit school district in all counties in which it was in operation.

Important agencies which were useful in the process of adaptation were: the officials of certain state and county offices; the national and state teachers associations; representatives of the United States Office of Education; the state school board association; local teachers' institutes; citizens' committees; mass meetings; prominent national, state, and local leaders; and editors of newspapers and magazines. The introduction of laws on the county-unit school district into the legislature appears to have acted as a device that assisted in diffusion of the adaptation.

The pattern of development which this adaptation follows differs from the local initiative patterns suggested by Cubberley and Mort in two important details. The idea of the county-unit school district in Utah does not appear to have originated from local sources and its diffusion was not assisted by the granting of any special financial aid by the state. Both of these differences probably are inherent in the fact that this adaptation was a change in the school organization itself, rather than an additional service to be offered by the school. Throughout the period of the diffusion of the county-unit school district, it followed the characteristic local initiative pattern with one exception—special aid.

SOME IMPLICATIONS OF THE STUDY

Although there is no attempt in this study to make direct application of the findings to situations in other states, certain implications of this study may not be inappropriate.

1. The attempt to secure consolidation of school districts by a majority vote of electors in each local school district does not find any support from the process of consolidation in Utah. The attempt to secure such consolidation by a majority vote of all the electors within the proposed consolidated district also gains little support from the experience in Utah.

2. If school district consolidation is secured by action of elected representatives of the people, the experience in Utah indicates that the action will soon be supported by popular approval. In this respect the action in Utah was not antidemocratic.

3. The experience in Utah indicates that this type of school organization should be tried out in a district that has strong leadership, that is in close proximity to a city having a similar type of organization, and that is undergoing a rapid growth in population and a needed expansion of school facilities.

4. Analysis of the process of development in Utah indicates that a large district organization is one of the persistent school needs and that there may be recurring periods of favorableness for achieving consolidation. The county-unit idea was first advocated in Utah as a means of securing graded elementary schools. Although the plan was widely advocated it was not achieved at that time. The next recurring need of a large district organization was that of the high school, and the county-unit district was adopted, to some degree at least, as a solution for that problem. It may be that the ability of leadership to use these recurring needs of school systems for the purpose of securing needed changes in district organization is the most important factor in the development of satisfactory units of school administration.

SUGGESTIONS FOR OTHER STUDIES

This study suggests the desirability of studying the process of voluntary adoptions already made in those states in which the adoption of the county-unit system is optional. Such studies may reveal certain common factors in the process of consolidation that would prove useful in accelerating the process of diffusion.

It would also seem desirable to study the status of the county unit in those states which have adopted it by mandatory law, to determine if a preliminary period of permissive legislation should precede a mandatory law in order to secure an efficient and popularly accepted system of county school districts.

BIBLIOGRAPHY

REFERENCES ON SOCIAL CHANGE

Allport, Floyd Henry. *Social Psychology.* Boston: Houghton Mifflin Co., 1924. pp. 260-291; 382-435.

Bogardus, Emory S. *Fundamentals of Social Psychology* (second edition). New York: The Century Co., 1931. pp. 358-372.

Bogardus, Emory S., ed. *Social Problems and Social Processes.* Chicago: University of Chicago Press, 1932. Part III, pp. 101-151.

Bristol, L. M. *Social Adaptation.* Cambridge: Harvard University Press, 1915. Parts IV and V, pp. 221-333.

Chapin, F. Stuart. *Cultural Change.* New York: The Century Co., 1928. Parts III and IV, pp. 201-439.

Hart, Hornell. *The Technique of Social Progress.* New York: Henry Holt and Co., 1931. 708 pp.

MacIver, R. M. *Society.* New York: Farrar and Rinehart, 1937. Part III, pp. 391-531.

Mort, Paul R. and Cornell, Francis G. *Adaptability of Public School Systems.* New York: Bureau of Publications, Teachers College, Columbia University, 1938. 146 pp.

Ogburn, W. F. *Social Change.* New York: Viking Press, 1928. 365 pp.

Sorokin, Pitirim. *Social Mobility.* New York: Harper & Bros., 1927. Part VI, pp. 493-547.

GENERAL REFERENCES ON UTAH AND THE COUNTY UNIT

No attempt has been made to include references on the theory of the county-unit school district or its status in other states. Good bibliographies for these phases of the subject may be found in the Monahan reference for 1914, the Nuttall reference for 1928, and the Deffenbaugh reference for 1933 in the following material.

Bancroft, Hubert Howe. *History of Utah.* San Francisco, 1889.

Cubberley, E. P. *The History of Education.* Boston: Houghton Mifflin Co., 1920.

Cubberley, E. P. *State School Administration.* Boston: Houghton Mifflin Co., 1927.

Deffenbaugh, Walter and Covert, Timon. *School Administrative Units with Special Reference to the County-Unit.* United States Office of Education, Pamphlet No. 34. Washington, D. C.: Government Printing Office, 1933. 25 pp.

Graves, Frank P. "State and County School Administration," Chapter X, pp. 299-326, in *Modern School Administration*, John C. Almack, editor. Boston: Houghton Mifflin Co., 1933.

Monahan, A. C. *County-Unit Organization for the Administration of Rural Schools*. U. S. Bureau of Education, Bulletin No. 44. Washington, D. C.: Government Printing Office, 1914. 56 pp.

Nuttall, L. John, Jr. *Progress in Adjusting Differences of Amount of Educational Opportunity Offered under the County-Unit Systems of Maryland and Utah*. New York: Bureau of Publications, Teachers College, Columbia University, 1931. 105 pp.

Parratt, J. Easton. "Legal Development of the Organization and Administration of the Public Schools of Utah." Unpublished Master's thesis. University of Chicago, 1928.

Young, Levi Edgar. *Dr. John Rocky Park*. Salt Lake City (no publisher given), 1919. 54 pp.

SCHOOL REPORTS

New Jersey. *Annual Report of the Board of Education and of the Superintendent of Public Instruction of New Jersey*, 1894. Appendix.

New York. *Thirty-fifth Annual Report of the Superintendent of Public Instruction of the State of New York*, 1889. Appendix.

Utah. *Biennial Reports of the Territorial Superintendent of Common Schools*, for the biennial periods ending in 1867 to 1875, inclusive.

Utah. *Biennial Reports of the Superintendent of District Schools for the Territory of Utah*, for the biennial periods ending in 1877 to 1883, inclusive.

Utah. *Biennial Reports of the Commissioner of Schools for Utah Territory*, for the biennial periods ending in 1887 to 1895, inclusive.

Utah. *First Report of the Superintendent of Public Instruction of the State of Utah*, for the school year ending June 30, 1896.

Utah. *Reports of the Superintendent of Public Instruction of the State of Utah* (second to eleventh reports, inclusive) for the biennial periods ending June 30, 1898 to June 30, 1916, inclusive.

Utah. *Report of the County Superintendent of District Schools of Salt Lake County, Utah*, July 1, 1907.

STATUTES AND LEGISLATIVE JOURNALS

The official statutes were used for reference because compilations of the school laws of Utah were not issued regularly and because this study, in certain years, required reference to the organization and authority of county and city governments.

Statutes

Compiled Laws of Utah, 1855, 1866, 1876, 1888.

Revised Statutes of Utah, 1898, 1907.

Session Laws of the Legislature of Territory of Utah, 1884, 1890, and 1892.

Session Laws of the Legislature of the State of Utah, 1897, 1901, 1905, 1907, 1909, 1911, 1913, and 1915.

Legislative Journals

Journal of the Legislative Assembly of the Territory of Utah, for the Sessions of 1854-55, 1878, 1888, and 1890.

House Journals of the Sessions of the Legislature of the State of Utah, for the Sessions of 1897, 1901, 1903, 1905, 1911, 1913, and 1915.

Senate Journals of the Sessions of the Legislature of the State of Utah, for the Sessions of 1905, 1911, 1913, and 1915.

COUNTY AND SCHOOL DISTRICT RECORDS

Journals of meetings of County Commissions (called County Court prior to 1896) in the following Utah counties:

Beaver, 1881	Millard, 1878, 1913-	Tooele, 1913-1915
Boxelder, 1905-1907	1915	Uintah, 1911-1915
Cache, 1863, 1864,	Morgan, 1905-1908	Utah, 1875, 1905-1915
1872, 1905-1911	Salt Lake, 1904-1905	Wasatch, 1910-1915
Carbon, 1913-1915	Sanpete, 1905-1915	Washington, 1877
Davis, 1907-1911	Sevier, 1905-1915	Weber, 1877-78, 1905
Juab, 1909-1915	Summit, 1911-1915	

Journals of meetings of County Boards of Education in the following Utah counties:

Boxelder, 1907-1908	Davis, 1908	Sevier, 1912
Cache, 1908-1911	Morgan, 1908	Weber, 1905

Newspapers

Boxelder News, Brigham City, Utah, May-June, 1907.

Carbon County News, Price, Utah, 1914.

Davis County Clipper, Kaysville, Utah, May, 1907; February-March, 1908; June-July, 1911.

Deseret Evening News, Salt Lake City, Utah, January-March, 1888; February-March, 1890; 1903-1905; January-March, 1915.

Ephraim Enterprise, Ephraim, Utah, April, 1908; April-November, 1911.

Manti Messenger, Manti, Utah. March-September, 1909; December, 1911; January-March, 1912.

Ogden Standard, Ogden, Utah, January, 1903; March-July, 1905.

Progress-Review, Fillmore, Utah, March-December, 1913.

Salt Lake Tribune, Salt Lake City, Utah, 1904-1905; January-March, 1915.

The Journal, Logan, Utah, February, 1908 to April, 1911.

Periodicals

Utah Educational Review. Vols. 1-8, 1907-1915.
Numerous editorial comments and news notes in reference to the county-unit school district appear in these volumes, in addition to the following articles:

> Burton, H. C. "Consolidation as a Socializing Power," Vol. 8, No. 9-10, p. 28, May-June, 1915.
>
> Matheson, A. C. "Consolidation of School Districts," Vol. 8, No. 9-10, pp. 6-13, May-June, 1915.
>
> Moss, James E. "B. W. Ashton," Vol. 7, No. 5-6, p. 51, January-February, 1914.
>
> Roylance, W. G. "The Consolidation of Schools and Education," Vol. 8, No. 9-10, pp. 5-6, May-June, 1915.
>
> Thomas, Mathonihah. "President's Address to Utah Education Association," Vol. 4, No. 6, pp. 10-12, February, 1911.

MISCELLANEOUS REFERENCES

Church of Jesus Christ of Latter Day Saints, Report, 1905, 1910, and 1915. Church Historian's Office, Salt Lake City, Utah.

Supreme Court of the Territory of Utah, Reports of Cases from January 1889 to June 1890. John M. Zane, reporter. Vol. VI. Chicago: Callaghan and Co., 1892.

United States Census Reports:
> Twelfth Census, 1900.
>
> Thirteenth Census, 1910.

Utah State Attorney General, Report for Biennial Period ending November 30, 1914.

Utah State Board of Equalization, Report, 1909-1910.